BEER SNOBS ARE BORING:

6 STEPS
TO DECODE YOUR PALATE
AND FEEL SMART ABOUT BEER
WITHOUT BEING BULLIED
BY BEER SNOBS

By Dale Thomas Vaughn

Shae Vaughn

Daniel Halleck

Copyright © 2015

Dale Thomas Vaughn, Shae Vaughn, Daniel Halleck

Foreword

Beer Snobs Are Boring

First kisses. That new job. Anniversaries. Moments of celebration. Toasts. Roasts. Our biggest moments in life are usually punctuated with a glass of something alcoholic.

Did you know that every ancient culture on Earth except the Australian aborigines had independently discovered and produced some form of alcohol? More than anything, this shared experience ties humanity together across borders of race, nationality and even religion.

When something good is happening, it's time to raise a glass! But what if you don't enjoy the drink in your glass? Are you missing out on something deeper?

We wrote this book to give you the knowledge you need to make sure your glass is always full of something you like.

We created a 3-step repeatable system that you can use to determine the right beer for anyone's palate.

According to the old pescetarian idiom… we're here to teach you to fish. If you use this book, you will never feel lost or bullied by a beer snob again.

This is a companion to ***Wine Snobs Are Boring***. When I wrote that book about wine, it was from a place of wanting to give people a repeatable system to find the right wine for their palate. I heard so many touching stories about how that book and system simplified and therefore opened up a complex world for people. So I called up my two cousins, Shae and Daniel, both burgeoning beer experts, and we decided to create a follow up about beer.

Thus ***Beer Snobs Are Boring*** was born.

This book is a somewhat rebellious, definitely precocious guide to unlearning the myths and misperceptions that may have held you back from experiencing the deepest pleasure of your palate.

This book is about you.

This book is about the tangible tactics of beer, you will learn what you like, how to get the most out of a tasting experience, and you will learn answers to those questions you sometimes feel foolish for Googling after a run-in with a snob.

About the Authors

We are a writing team of 3 cousins. When I started to dream up the "Snobs are Boring" franchise, I knew I could write the wine edition alone; but that I would need help with the beer edition. I reached out to my cousins because they know more about beer than I do, and because we like meeting with each other (virtually) to create this project. It has been a fun process, and I hope you enjoy our collaborative product. - Dale

About Dale Thomas Vaughn

Inventor of the unique P.A.L.A.T.E. system which debuted in "Wine Snobs Are Boring" - his first of 5 best-selling books on Amazon.

He is a Certified Specialist of Wine by the Society of Wine Educators, a writer at the American Winery Guide for California's Central Coast, and a co-founder of a small backyard vineyard in north Texas. He has studied and traveled in France, Spain, Italy, Germany, Portugal, and the United States, specializing in the Santa Barbara Valley of California.

About Shae Vaughn

Cicerone Certified Beer Server

Just a southern gentleman and business professional, his beer odyssey began like others with his first beer passed to him by none other than Dale Thomas Vaughn at a family gathering. Since then he attended Texas A&M University and after graduating has become a

Cicerone Certified Beer Server, having both tasted hundreds of beers and served them to thousands. Next on his list is to join the fraternity of brewers and travel the globe and continue his odyssey.

About Daniel Halleck

Gentleman and Scholar

Curious beer drinker. Lower 48 traveler. Collegiate athlete. Aspiring brewer. By day he helps people in their technical difficulties, by night he leads a mission to educate the masses about truly great beer.

Also by Dale Thomas Vaughn

FICTION
Fatal Breach

Action/adventure novel about purpose, fate, romance, brotherhood, and holding on to the seat of your pants.

Dr. Mann's Kind Folly
AMAZON BEST-SELLER

A sci-fi novella about Dr. Mann, a time-traveling, jetpacking, mad scientist in an intense moral dilemma.

NON-FICTION
Wine Snobs Are Boring
AMAZON BEST-SELLER

Identify your unique wine palate so you are never lost in the wine aisle or stressed by the wine menu ever again.

The 10-Minute Memoir
AMAZON BEST-SELLER

This book came from a deep heartfelt desire to know the stories of my family. Write Your Memoir In Just 10 Minutes A Day With This Easy Q&A Journal

Connect with Us

Dale:

www.Facebook.com/DaleThomasVaughn

or

www.Twitter.com/NextGent

Shae:

Twitter.com/VaughnS13

Daniel:

Twitter.com/SouthernYankie9

Your Thoughts

We love hearing from our readers so please feel free to reach me and to leave a review here on my Amazon page:

www.amazon.com/author/dalethomasvaughn

Beer Snobs Are Boring
6 STEPS
TO DECODE YOUR PALATE
AND FEEL SMART ABOUT BEER
WITHOUT BEING BULLIED
BY BEER SNOBS

Published 2015 by Dale Thomas Vaughn, Shae Vaughn, Daniel Halleck

This book is licensed for your personal enjoyment and education only. While best efforts have been used, the author and publisher are not offering legal, accounting, medical, or any other professional services advice and make no representations or warranties of any kind and assume no liabilities of any kind with respect to the accuracy or completeness of the contents and specifically disclaim any implied warranties of merchantability or fitness of use for a particular purpose, nor shall they be held liable or responsible to any person or entity with respect to any loss or incidental or consequential damages caused, or alleged to have been caused, directly or indirectly, by the information or programs contained herein. Stories, characters, and entities are fictional. Any likeness to actual persons, either living or dead, is strictly coincidental.

If this book provides wellness, health, and fitness management information it is done in an educational manner only, with information that is general in nature and that is not specific to you, the reader. The contents are intended to assist you and other readers in your personal wellness efforts. Nothing in this book should be construed as personal advice or diagnosis, and must not be used in this manner. The information in this book should not be considered as complete and does not cover all diseases, ailments, physical conditions, or their treatment. You should consult with your physician regarding the applicability of any information provided herein and before beginning any exercise, weight loss, or health care program.

All rights reserved. No part of this publication may be reproduced or transmitted in any form or by any means, electronic or mechanical, including photocopying, recording, or by any information storage and retrieval system, without permission in writing from the publisher. All images are free to use or share, even commercially, according to Google at the time of publication unless otherwise noted. Thank you for respecting the hard work of the author(s) and everyone else involved.

Copyright © 2015
Dale Thomas Vaughn, Shae Vaughn, Daniel Halleck

Authors and sources cited throughout retain the copyright to their respective materials.

Dedication

Thank you to my family and friends. Without you life would be boring. Thank you for your love and support through all the laughs in the good times and picking me up during the bad times. Thank you to my Papaw for teaching me how to be a man of honor, duty, faith, and dedicated to one's family. Also to my dearest mother for always believing in me, showing me what true strength, courage, and love is.

- Shae

I'd like to thank my mom, dad, sisters, extended family and brewmates for letting me pick their brains in a creation of this book. I couldn't have done it without you.

- Daniel

Thank you to Grandpa Dunkelberg for inspiring a group of dispersed family to stay in touch through the decades. This book was borne from a foundation of a lifetime of campfires. In many ways, this book is a product of the first fraternity: family.

- Dale

"Beer,

if drunk in moderation,

softens the temper,

cheers the spirit

and promotes health."

- Thomas Jefferson

Contents

Foreword	6
About the Authors	9
Contents	23
Introduction	25
Chapter One	31
Chapter Two - The Best Way to Learn Beer	37
Chapter Three - P is for Palate	41
Chapter Four - A is for Ask	53
The Most Commonly Asked Beer Questions	55
Choosing the Best Beer for you	70
Keeping and Serving Beer	78
Chapter Five - L is for Love	89
Chapter Six - A is for Adventure	119
A brief history of beer!	127
Chapter Seven - T is for Technical	133

Chapter Eight - E is for Education   **155**

Interesting Facts To Stump the Snobs   **165**

References   **173**

Introduction

"He was a wise man who invented beer."

Plato

Gold, pale, black, amber, brown and red. Beer comes in many colors and just as many flavors, tastes and names. The nectar of the gods. Or better yet, the beverage of mankind.

It can be thick and heavy, or clear and light as a feather. It can be full of flavor meant to have every drop savored and consumed slowly, or be guzzled with gusto in celebration. There is a beer for every occasion and mood.

Beer is one of the oldest beverages on the planet coming in at over ten thousand years old. Countless generations have brewed, evolved, and enjoyed this beverage through the ages. Brewing is a punctuation of the advance of agriculture as well as technology. The industry creates jobs, fills people's bellies, quenches thirst, and brings cheer.

While earning billions in revenue a year, beer is a drink that both the rich and the poor, young and old can enjoy. It is my favorite beverage and one that I have grown to love. It is more than something I consume. It is a hobby, a job and a passion.

I enjoy a brewski on my own, or as a link that connects me to friends and family. An ale is more than a drink. It is part of the human experience. No two beers are alike, similar to fingerprints. If those were not reasons enough as to why I love beer so much, then here is another: beer brings people together.

You can see why I love beer so much, but why write a book about it? I want you to open that next bottle or drink that next pint with more knowledge than the last time you had one.

I want you to taste the flavors both painstakingly and passionately added. Inhale the aromas of the hops, yeast, malt, and other ingredients. Feel the tickle of foam on a perfectly poured head of beer.

I want you to be able to walk into the beer aisle at your liquor store, supermarket, or brewpub and not stare blankly into oblivion at all the choices or quake in your shoes from fear of not knowing what to look for. Or heaven forbid make a hasty or uneducated decision on a less than ideal fit for you.

More importantly I want you to gain knowledge that you too might be able to spread to your friends and family.

I was approached to write this book in order to spread my knowledge of the beer industry. Yet, where does one begin?

With this book, I hope to start you on your path to the promised land of beer, and to take away your zythophobia (fear of beer).

If you have already begun your journey or have gotten lost in it, this book will help to steer you and your palate onto the path. And the best place to start is simple, and that is by popping a top off of a cold one while you read this book.

Chapter One
Origin Stories

"I would give all my fame for a pot of ale" -
Shakespeare, Henry V

We thought you might like to get to know us a little bit… and so we'll start at the beginning. Our first beers and when we knew we were going all in.

The Story of Shae

First, Mother and both of my Grandmothers if you are reading this section I am going to have to ask you to skip to the next chapter.

In the Beginning, it was my grandparents' 50th wedding anniversary, and the whole family was gathered for a grand weekend of celebration. I was in my early teenage years, definitely not of legal age, following my older cousins like a puppy watching and learning all I could. I remember one night in particular, staying up late listening to stories from older cousins, aunts, uncles, and grandparents of their glory years - when I received a life-altering gift.

My eldest cousin who I idolized, still do if truth be told, gave me my first true taste of the promised land. My first beer. Now like I said I was not of legal age to drink this beer so it was like being handed the forbidden fruit from Eden. He simply smiled at me, "It's ok, it'll be our secret." I held that can with the utmost care as I was in awe of the gift I had been given.

I inspected the can carefully wanting to memorize every detail of this moment. It came in a red and white aluminum can with the words Budweiser printed on the side. It was golden, fizzed with carbonation, and was ice cold. I remember every sip because in the mind of this young teenager it tasted... TERRIBLE. That particular can of beer tasted like I was drinking sparkling bread. This teenager did not touch another beer for many years.

The next time I would give beer another try would be the summer before leaving for college. To celebrate my graduation, several friends and I got together not to throw a party but to enjoy our first collegiate beer together in send-off fashion. I would pop the top of another well known brew in a green bottle with two large red Xs on the side.

This one tasted significantly better than the first beer I tried, especially with a lime. Yet, it did not bring me running to the open arms of beer lovers. This second taste was much different than the first. Not only for the fact that the beers were different but my focus and knowledge was different.

Budweiser and Dos XX taste significantly different, yet when I tried the first brew I had no previous experience to go off of. It was a whole new world, anything was possible. With the second tasting I knew more as well as what to expect when trying a new brew. Though I had yet to have an epiphany beer that would openly bring me into the beer drinking world.

Onward into my college days, filled like all other college students with gratuitous amounts of beer - I mean studying, yes of course, studying. Many fraternity and sorority parties, thirsty thursdays, friday nights, saturday college game days, and just random tuesday nights. How many gallons of cheap ice cold beer we consumed.

In the beginning like any poor college student I drank whatever cheap beer I could get my hands on; Keystone Light, Natural Lite, Busch, Malt 40oz beers because it was cool thing to do not because we knew anything about beer. If we actually had money in our pockets then we'd treat ourselves big and get Budweiser, Miller Lite, Coors, Dos XXs, or Texas' own Shiner Bock.

With each new beer I tried I learned more and more, and began developing my palate. No longer did every beer cost, taste, look, or smell the same. I had broken through the initial barriers of displeasure, misconceptions, and lack of knowing my palate.

Finally, we come to the present. I bring my beer experiences to where I am today. Now that I'm a functioning adult in society, or at least like to think I am, with a little bit of money in my pocket. I can afford the finer things in life such as developing my beer palate still further.

I wanted something more from my beer. I wanted to experience other cultures through their brewing without leaving the comfort of home. I wanted to learn about craft beer and what all the hullabaloo was about.

All the experience I have beginning with that first beer with my cousins brought me to where I am today. I went from zero knowledge to a great understanding of my palate as well as beer's history and techniques and the industry itself.

I started off small with light mainstream industrialized American beer and have worked my way up into the craft beer movement where no one beer is the same and even if it is the same beer each batch has new identities. With the craft beer movement in full swing, trying any and all brews, the sky's the limit.

Your taste buds change as you age, what you once hated as a child you may love as an adult. I began despising Budweiser, an American Adjunct Lager, and I have now grown to appreciate Budweiser and to love Brown Ales, Belgian Ales, Stouts, and Wheat Beers. Lambics and Sours have yet to grow on me but maybe one day.

Exotic and seasonal brews may come and go, but beer stays eternal.

The Story of Daniel

For the majority of people getting into the craft beer scene, the conversation usually sounds like this:

"Man, you gotta try this."

"What is it?"

"Oh it's their new IPA."

I personally got tired of this conversation. So after several months of people only talking about the bitter hoppy IPAs, I started my beer odyssey.

I started with wheat. Most macro breweries play commercials on repeat with golden beers, golden bubbles and golden tan girls bouncing around. We all know that the girls don't exist, but it turns out the bubbles do. I started by ordering a new beer each time I was at a bar. I forced myself to never have the same beer twice.

This process of ordering a new beer every time I had the opportunity led me through amber lagers, ales, porters and stouts. The more I tasted the more I liked. It grew from a small hobby into a form of customer service. When I sit down at the bar with a friend, they ask me "What are you drinking tonight, Dan?"

I still consider myself a novice in the subject because there's so much to learn, but hopefully the documentation of our odyssey will help you along yours.

The Story of Dale

To me, beer equals grandfathers.

My Grandaddy would let me sip the foam from a fresh Budweiser if I brought him one - which is a nifty life hack. Since he was a legend to me, I assumed beer was what great men drink. I still can drink a Budweiser and remember the feelings of wonder that exist between the magical grandfather and grandson.

It wasn't until I was 16 that I had my first full beer, from my other grandfather, for medicinal purposes. See, I had tried a hot sauce that made me sweat from my eyes, and he took pity on me by handing me a Coors. This was out of character for him, but I could tell it was his way of saying - "here, beer will make everything better."

I spent time in college and in Europe drinking whatever was cheap. After learning how wine could be better with education and diversity of experience, I began applying that pattern to beer.

Since I visited the Hofbrau tent in Munich during Oktoberfest, I've been mainly a fan of darker ales and strong lagers, but I know there are more beers out there.

Some of my Favorites:

- Smithwicks
- Allagash Curieux
- Spaten Lager
- Chimay Red
- Fuller's ESB

Chapter Two
The Best Way to Learn Beer

*"If God had intended us to drink beer,
He would have given us stomachs."*

— *David Daye*

I invented the PALATE method to learn wine for beginners… and it turns out it works for beer (and other books, upcoming) as well.

Here's a quick understanding of what we'll cover.

If you had time and you were at my bar, or sitting at my dinner table, I'd start by helping you to discern your **Palate** (Chapter 3) and what you will probably like, then I'd help you **Ask** all of the most common questions about finding, buying, storing, and caring for beer (Chapter 4), then I'd help you learn how to actually **Love** the act of tasting the beer in your glass (Chapter 5), then I'd help you make a plan for your **Adventure** through new beer styles and traditions (Chapter 6), then I'd get into the **Technical** aspect of brewing (Chapter 7), and then I'd talk to you about how to get further **Education** if you really wanted it (Chapter 8).

This is basically the way I learned wine and beer over about 13 years of trial and error… just condensed and served to you in safe, approachable chapters.

Instead of being bullied by the "experts" through ratings, reviews, and even by the availability of a relatively small selection of variety… you get to skip forward and confidently stride to the bar with a style and profile that will make the Hop Head behind the bar shake in his boots because you know what you like before he can tell you what he thinks you *should* like.

The PALATE Program

Step

1 **P**alate — Your unique palate is as important as anyone else's.

2 **A**sk — Learn how to ask questions to get and learn what you like.

3 **L**ove — Discover how to love the beer in your glass in the moment.

4 **A**dventure — Plan how to explore the areas at the edges of your map.

5 **T**echnical — The technical side of tasting and understanding beer.

6 **E**ducation — Find where you can learn more about beer... if you want to.

Chapter Three
P is for Palate

Identifying Your Unique Palate

"Isn't beer the holy libation of sincerity? The potion that dispels all hypocrisy, any charade of fine manners?"

- *Milan Kundera*
Author of The Unbearable Lightness of Being

One of the joys of my life is introducing people to their own palate. Over the years I've perfected the Palate Identity Program that has helped hundreds of people learn about their own palate by answering a few non-beer-related questions. You will get a chance to go through this program right now and determine the identity of your palate.

Answer the following three questions, after which you will be given a Palate Identity number and a profile…

The Index has a comprehensive list of beers you'll want to try.

Once you have your Palate Identity, you will have all of the secret code words you will need to get the right beers for you. You'll have a map of places to explore and styles to seek. You'll know how to describe yourself with confidence when you approach a bar, restaurant, or pesky snob at a party.

You'll have so much confidence that you'll quickly learn how boring all of the snobs are.

Sound good? Ready?

Give yourself a rating on each of the following pages… and remember, just because there are numbers, doesn't mean there are grades. No one palate is better than another, so answer as honestly as you can and see what happens.

	Question 1: How do you take your coffee/tea?		
10	I Don't Like Coffee or Tea		Why be bitter when I can be sweet?
20	Caramel Frappuccino	Green Tea Smoothie with sweetener	I like coffee ice cream and tiramisu, does that count?
30	If coffee, 4+ spoons of sweetener and half-n-half	Sweet Tea	I can make coffee or tea work for me, but I'd prefer a soda
40	Frappucino, but no flavoring	Long Island Iced Tea	Cold and fun to drink is best for me
50	Mocha Latte	Mint or Green Tea	I like layered flavors - coffee or tea both need complimentary layers
60	Latte	Two Packets/spoons of sweetener	Sweetness isn't as important as softness, temperature and color
70	Cappucino	Iced Tea no sweetener	Dash of Almond or Coconut Milk
80	A little cream	Macchiato	You should see my fancy Tea collection - Yerba Mate, white tea, ginger... you name it
90	Espresso	Black Tea	Does Espresso Stout count?
100	Black Drip Coffee from a diner if possible	Turkish Coffee	I drink lukewarm Mud for breakfast, fear me

Question 2 : Which would you choose?	
50	Dark Chocolate
40	Grapefruit
30	Chocolate Orange
20	Lemon Meringue Pie
10	Crisp Apple

Question 3: What kind of Bread do you like for breakfast?	
50	Sour Dough
40	Bagel
30	Croissant
20	Chocolate Croissant
10	French Toast/pancakes
0	Donut

Now add up your total scores from question 1, 2, and 3 and you will have your PALATE IDENTITY number. Next you will find all you need to understand about your palate to begin or enhance your journey into wine.

The Palate Identity Profiles

Total PALATE Score = 1 Through 40

Flavor Profile: "Light and Refreshing"

You may not love the bitter taste of beer, but you may like the refreshing feel and effect of beer. You are lucky, because you account for the majority of the advertising budgets of all the big brewers in the world. You are fun at a party and you are not a snob about your beer. You like ice cold brews on a hot day. You probably have a brand you stick with because to you that's what beer is supposed to taste like. **If you get stuck**, *just ask for something "light and refreshing."* **If you want to branch out**, *try amber lagers, European style pilsners, and lambic beers like Framboise.*

Your Secret Code words: Light, refreshing, ice cold, maybe even floral or sweet if you're adventurous.

Your Beer Styles: Pilsner, pale lager, light beer, Lambic, Kolsch, Cider

Some brands for you: Corona/Bud/Coors/Miller Lite, Fosters, Molson's, Strongbow (cider), Sapporo, Tsingtao, Peroni, Stella Artois, Kronenbourg, Pilsner Urquell, Rolling Rock, Modelo Especial

Total PALATE Score = 41 Through 80

Flavor Profile: "Citrus and Gold"

You prefer beers to be crisp and smooth. You graduated from light beers and found your favorites have just a little more flavor. You are right at home in a German biergarten and an English pub. You can probably handle more bitter beers, but you really prefer something that feels and tastes festive. You love the smell of baking bread. You love the slight touch of citrus on the palate. You drink beer and ale the way they were originally intended. ***If you get stuck****, just ask for something crisp and golden.* ***If you want to branch out****, try a cream ale or a brown ale.*

Your Secret Code words: Golden or light amber color, crisp and smooth, wheat, and you like some sourness or citrus (maybe even an added lime or orange a la Blue Moon)

Styles for You: Vienna Lager, Hefeweizen, Belgian Wit/Wheat, Sour Ale, Blond Ale, Pale Ale (NOT India Pale Ale)

Brands for You: Spaten Lager, Sam Adams Boston Lager, Hofbrau Hefeweizen, Blue Moon, Dos Equis, Dale's Pale Ale, Yuengling Red Lager, Shock Top, Pranqster, Heineken, Paulaner, Carlsberg, Weihenstephaner, Czechvar Pilsner, Leffe

Total PALATE Score = 81 Through 120

Flavor Profile: "Toffee, Nuts and Malts"

You like subtle power and simple genuine joys. You might like Snickers bars and the smell of roasted chestnuts. You like a lot of different styles of beer, but you prefer a moderate ale with a good balance. You like beer that tells a changing story, but one that is always pleasant. You like complex aromas and flavors and you get bored with beer styles that all taste the same. ***If you get stuck****, ask for a good brown ale.* ***If you want to branch out****, start playing with Oktoberfest beers.*

Secret Code Words: sophisticated, caramel colored, not too hoppy, good balance, good caramel and/or toasted malt

Styles for You: Belgian Ale, Marzen/Oktoberfest, Bocks, Brown Ale, Belgian Golden Ale, Winter Ales (not Christmas Ales)

Brands for You: Newcastle, Hofbrau Oktoberfest, Spaten Oktoberfest, Shiner Bock, Sam Smith's Nut Brown Ale, Sam Adams, Negra Modelo, Fuller's ESB, Boddington's Pub Ale, Spaten Optimator

Total PALATE Score = 121 Through 160

Flavor Profile: "Dark Roasted Richness"

You enjoy highly roasted malts and grains for deep coffee and cocoa flavors. You like rich mouthfeels, and copper to very dark colors. You love the smell of coffee and toasted bread or hazelnuts. You can hang with anything, but you really love the depth of a complicated dark beer. You like the ripe fruit accents from a good Belgian as much as you like the dark chocolate and espresso notes of a robust porter. **If you get stuck**, *ask for something dark.* **If** *you want to branch out*, try an Imperial Stout, a smoked porter, a quadruple, or anything aged in strange barrels (whiskey, port, coffee, etc.).

Secret Codewords: Dark, Roasted, Smoky, Espresso, Chocolate, Belgian Style, Red

Styles for You: Stout, Porter, Scottish Ale, Red Ale, Dubbels/Tripels

Brands for You: Guinness, Smithwicks, Chimay, Murphy's, La Fin Du Monde, Allagash Curieux, Brother Thelonious, Maredsous, Belhaven, Sam Smith Taddy Porter, LeTrappe

Total PALATE Score = 161 Through 200

Flavor Profile: "Hints of fruit and lots of Earthiness"

You like depth, you like darkness, you like challenge... we're not talking about life, we're talking about taste. You will always be the one at the table who asks to pass the pepper. You like steak, blackened fish, and bacon. The new craft beer world is set up to make sure you have a beer on every list for you, which is good, because *you know a lot more about beer than most of your friends. **If you get stuck**, just ask for the most hoppy and complex beer on the menu. **If you want to branch out**, try barleywines and local experimental beers.*

Your Secret Codewords: Hoppy, powerful, robust, complicated, high ABV

Styles for You: IPA, Double IPA, Imperial IPA, Quadrupels, Barleywine, Mead

Brands for You: Chimay Blue, Maredsous 10, Gulden Draak, Stone, Lagunitas IPA, Ballast Point, Russian River Brewing Company, Tree House Brewing Company, Harpoon, Goose Island, Ommegang, St. Arnold's, Karbach, Real Ale Brewery, Deschutes, Black Butte, Smithwicks barleywine, Sierra Nevada "Bigfoot"

You now have a Palate Identity number and profile, keep this in mind as we go forward. This simple profile can unlock the entire beer world and experience to you. In the next chapter we'll teach you how to employ this new knowledge in real world situations, and we'll answer all of the most frequently asked questions about beer so you can feel confident while you ask yours.

Chapter Four
A is for Ask

How to ask for what you want, and the answers to the questions you have always wanted to ask, but didn't.

"I got 99 problems & beer solves them all"
- Earl Dibbles Jr. aka Granger Smith

You now have a Palate Identity number and profile that tells you how you like your body, flavors, and some styles you'll want to ask for at your next opportunity… but how exactly do you make sure you're getting what you want specifically? You'll need to ask the right questions.

This can be terrifying because you've been bullied into thinking there are stupid questions. Below is a list of the most commonly asked questions about beer, and their answers. You'll find that you probably know a lot of them already, but you'll also find some fun and exciting answers to the questions that may have stumped you for years.

Before we get to those questions though, it's important to note that the brewing culture has certain vocabulary that is completely esoteric.

You can either cower in a corner at the sound of lingo like "robust, caramelized, nutty, or hoppy;" or you can get in the game and make your own words up. This is a medium based entirely on sharing personal perspective and opinion, so take creative control and see if you can enjoy the interplay of making up your own sensual language around beer.

When asking for a brewski to suit your palate, start by using some of the identifiers from your Palate Identity number. If you're a 150, say something like, "do you have any complex dark roasted malt ales with good body and some mild bitterness? I like Porters, Scottish Ales, and Dubbels/Tripels, but I'm also open to stouts and red ales." You'll knock the bartender over.

Seriously. You'd be surprised what asking for what you want can do for you. If the brewer or bartender comes back with something outside of what you specifically asked for, you can feel free to quiz him/her on the qualities of the brew. This is a great way to learn new exciting things about beer, and a great way to feel confident while experiencing it. As an exercise, write down a fictional conversation with a brewer, bartender, or liquor store beer snob wherein you state what you want and then get to feel empowered and in control of the situation. Use your Palate Identity number to help you with your opening line.

The Most Commonly Asked Beer Questions

These questions were carefully collected from multiple websites and by polling my beer snob friends about what they usually get asked. I've collected them into relevant categories to help you have a cleaner and more direct approach to understanding them.

Ales vs. Lagers?

Do you want to take the red or blue pill? Or in our case do you want to drink an Ale or a Lager. This isn't the matrix, or is it, but beer falls into two major categories. Ale or Lager. The two branches of the brewing tree, with all the beer styles growing from one or the other.

Ales are like the Catholic Church, the the first christian religion till a schism was led and Lagers were born. Beer begins with Ales. They are the first brews to come about dating back as far as the Egyptians, Sumerians, and Kurdistan.

What makes a beer an ale or a Lager? The difference between the two resides in fermentation. Ales are warm fermented as well as top fermented. This means that during fermentation when the yeast is munching on the delicious sugars of the wort, the remnants of the yeast rise to the top of the fermentation tanks. The duration of the fermentation of Ales is fast and ranges based upon the style but typically runs about three to ten days and can be as little as seven. Also the fermentation temperature is considered warm because unlike Lagers, ales are not cooled or chilled during fermentation by refrigeration but naturally cools due to the warehouse or cellar.

Another difference between an Ale or a Lager is that of the yeast strain that is used, *Saccharomyces Cerevisiae*. The typical indicators of an Ale outside of fermentation is their higher ABV rating and complex aromas. Other indicators from tasting include strong, assertive, and more robust notes of malt as well as spicy, fruity estery flavors.

      I'd bet a lot of money that a majority of Americans probably drank a lager as their first beer. This is in part due to the Lager being dulled down to fit the widest range of beer drinkers available, due to massive commercial marketing and the cheapness of the product the Lager has become *lowbrow* beer. Yet from a tasting perspective this is just not true. Any beer if made incorrectly is bad beer, a beer is not bad simply because of the style.

      The first Lager ever brewed is unknown, but the location is said to be in Munich in the year 1420. Though by 1600, Bavaria was consuming Lager beer like water. So relatively speaking the Lager is young in age compared to the Ale which is several thousand years old. In the previous chapter we discussed what beer is and the manner in which it is created.

      Yet what makes a brew a Lager? The difference between a Lager and an Ale lies not in the ingredients but the manner in which it is fermented. During fermentation yeast is added to the wort, the sugary liquid derived from boiling malt in water, but where does the yeast go? For the beer to be a Lager the yeast falls to the bottom of the tank.

This type of fermentation is called bottom or low fermentation. Bottom fermentation is also typically done cold or while chilling the brew.

This is where the Lager comes from, because a lager is cold bottom fermented and stored during brewing. The word Lager comes from German diction which means "storeroom or warehouse" where the brew was cold fermented.

Along with the location of fermentation in the tanks, the duration is another indicator of a Lager. The duration of fermentation in a Lager ranges depending on styles of the beer from a week to several months.

The final indicator during fermentation of a Lager is the strain of yeast used, *Saccharomyces Uvarum*. *Saccharomyces Uvarum* is the standard strain of most brewed lagers.

Several other indicators of a Lager include a lower ABV, high CO_2 levels, and more pronounced hops than compared to an Ale. Several examples of lager beer styles include, the American Lager, Oktoberfest Marzen, Kolsch, Bocks, Doppelbocks, Schwarzbier, and the Pilsner (the offspring of the Lager from Plzen, Czech. 1842) just to name a few.

When tasting a lager you will note that they are typically described as smoother, crisper, and more subtle than Ales.

Is beer healthy?

In moderation, beer has multiple health benefits.

Not least of importance, beer filters water. Alcoholic beverages have been invented in almost every ancient culture on Earth because of the lack of safety in drinking water. Water breeds bacteria and communicable disease easily without proper filtration, which is where beer and wine first came to prominence. Generally speaking, if you travel, beer is always more safe to drink than local water.

If you are fortunate enough to live with clean water (unlike 780 million people on this planet according to WHO/UNICEF), and death from drinking water is not among your top concerns (unlike 3.4 million people who die from water-hygiene related causes every year); then what you may be asking is more like health-related justification points for drinking beer, so you can feel good about the glass in front of you, or so you can argue with your crazy in-laws.

In that case, here are the ways beer has been proven or suggested to benefit your health:

- In general, several authors have reported that in subjects consuming wine in moderation the risk of mortality from all causes is 20-30% lower than in abstainers.
- Polyphenols (byproducts typically associated with red wine, but also present in beer) help prevent damage to blood vessels, reduce low-density lipoprotein (LDL) cholesterol (the "bad" cholesterol) and prevent blood clots.

Neither the American Heart Association nor the National Heart, Lung, and Blood Institute recommend that you start drinking alcohol just to prevent heart disease. Alcohol can be addictive and can cause or worsen other health problems.

Drinking too much alcohol increases your risk of high blood pressure, high triglycerides, liver damage, obesity, certain types of cancer, accidents and other problems. In addition, drinking too much alcohol regularly can cause weakened heart muscle (cardiomyopathy), leading to symptoms of heart failure in some people.

However, hops, give beer its bitter taste while delivering what are called "bitter acids," which have an array of health-promoting effects including anti-inflammatory benefits, according to a 2009 laboratory study published in Molecular Nutrition and Food Research.

According to a 2013 funded by Japanese beer manufacturer Sapporo, one type of bitter acid, humulone, is shown to help in preventing and treating viral respiratory infections.

Bitter acids in beer may also improve digestion. A 2012 study published in the Journal of Agricultural and Food Chemistry looked at five types of German and Austrian beer and found that each triggered the release of gastric acid from stomach cells. The more bitter acids a brew contained, the greater the response. Gastric acid is key for both digesting food in the stomach and controlling the growth of dangerous gut bacteria.

Lots of chemicals found in beer have shown promise in preventing or even treating cancer — although studies so far have been in Petri dishes and rodents.

One type of bitter acid, lupulone, wiped out tumors in rats with colon cancer who consumed it in their drinking water, according to a 2007 study published in Carcinogenesis. Xanthohumol, another beer ingredient, also looks promising.

A 2010 study by an Austrian research team found that xanthohumol shut down abnormal cell growth and prevented DNA damage in rats exposed to cancer-causing chemicals. The researchers say xanthohumol is likely to be good for humans too, since its cancer-fighting effects were seen at relatively low doses — equivalent to what people would get with moderate beer consumption.

Beer is a great source of silicon, which is important for building and maintaining healthy bones. In fact, the form of this mineral that's found in beer, orthosilicic acid, is extra easy for the body to metabolize, according to a 2013 report in the International Journal of Endocrinology. If you're looking for a brew that will build your bones, try an India pale ale. IPAs and other beers with lots of malted barley and hops are the best beer sources of silicon, according to a 2010 report from University of California, Davis researchers.

Huge studies have found a 25 percent lower risk of heart disease in people who drink from one-half to two drinks daily, compared to abstainers. And alcoholic beverages that are rich in polyphenols — think beer! — may be especially good for the heart, according to a 2012 research review.

Beer has benefits for people who already have heart disease, as well as for healthy folks. Men who had survived a heart attack were nearly half as likely to die over the next 20 years if they drank a couple of beers a day, Harvard researchers reported in 2012.

Xanthohumol — that chemical found in beer that can shrink liver tumors in rats — can also protect brain cells from oxidative damage, according to a 2015 study from China. Austrian researchers reported in 2013 that xanthohumol and other beer ingredients promoted the growth and development of neurons — in the lab.

A study in nearly 200,000 patients published in 2013 showed that while sugary soda and punch boosted kidney-stone risk, beer drinking reduced the likelihood of kidney stone formation by 60 percent. "Our study suggests that beer consumption is associated with reduced risk of forming stones in three large U.S. cohorts," says Pietro

Manuel Ferraro, MD, of the Catholic University of the Sacred Heart in Rome.[1]

Is beer gluten free/kosher/vegan?

Most beer contains gluten unless expressly labeled.

Gluten isn't necessarily bad, but some people are gluten-intolerant, meaning their bodies produce an abnormal immune response when it breaks down gluten from wheat and related grains during digestion.[2]

Most beer is vegan, or does not use animal products. Some British ale companies use animal products for filtration. If you need to be sure, PETA actually has a whole list of beers that are suitable for vegans.[3]

All unflavored beer with no additives are considered to be kosher, even without certification.[4]

How many calories are in a pint of ale?

---

[1] Secondary research from EverydayHealth.com
[2] From LiveScience.com
[3] www.peta.org/about-peta/faq/which-beers-are-suitable-for-vegans/
[4] According to the Chicago Rabbinical Council

Most beer is between 90 and 300 calories, with the large majority of what you see at a pub being between 140-220 calories. Your typical pale lager or pilsner will be around 140 calories. Ales vary wildly between 150-200, and some of the high alcohol beers can get up to 300 calories or above.

If you are counting calories, you are essentially looking to ration your alcohol.

The general scientific definition of a calorie is "the amount of heat required… to raise the temperature of one gram of water one degree celsius." So a calorie is essentially a unit of heat, and you have probably seen how well alcohol burns.

However, beer is a little bit different than other alcoholic drinks. Beer is not usually as alcoholic as wine, but can often have much higher calorie counts because of the amount of carbohydrates in beer.

What is beer foam?

Beer foam is called the "*head*" of the beer. This is the frothy stuff on top when the beer is poured. This is carbon dioxide rising to the surface. The head of the beer provides a lot of aroma. A correctly poured beer will have around an inch of foam. The size of the foam and the consistency depends on the style and serving glass.

How much alcohol does a glass beer constitute?

Knowing the alcohol content of a beer can be life-saving, night-making, or irrelevant... depending on your aims. Luckily, there are beer snobs who have made it easy for us to determine the amount of booze in our beers.

Alcohol by volume, or ABV%, tells us the portion of the total volume of liquid that is alcohol. To determine the ABV of a beer, a brewer uses a hydrometer, which measures the density of a liquid in relation to water. Through a series of equations related to the original gravity and the final gravity (which are measures of sugar), brewers can determine how much sugar has been transformed into alcohol by yeast during the fermentation of the wort (which is what beer is called before yeast is added to catalyze the spirity goodness).

Most beers you'll see contain between 5% to 14% alcohol by volume. By comparison wine is 12-15% and vodka/whiskey are typically around 40-50%.

Here are a few of the typical kinds of beer and their ABV:

- Lager: 4% to 5% alcohol by volume
- Pilsner: 3% to 6% alcohol by volume
- Stout: 5% to 10% alcohol by volume
- Porter: 4% to 5% alcohol by volume
- Brown Ale: 4% to 6% alcohol by volume
- Indian Pale Ale: 6% to 7% alcohol by volume

Occasionally you'll see ABW, which is alcohol by weight. If you see this, just assume it's 1-2% higher in alcohol than what it says… also, assume you're hanging out with beer snobs.

Why do some beers give me a headache?

The most common reason for headaches while drinking beer… is ALCOHOL.

The research suggests that excluding alcohol as the culprit, the true headache triggers in beer is the amino acid tyramine. Some doctors and researchers say taking anti-inflammatories, ibuprofen or motrin before you drink is effective in preventing headaches. But, remember, some people can have harmful reactions to the use of these over-the-counter drugs with alcohol, so ask your doctor first.

Drinking plenty of water when you're having a cold one might also help. Dehydration may also cause headaches, too.

How can I prevent a alcohol-induced hangover headache? If you experience a headache the day after drinking, there are some measures you can take to prevent the headache:

Step 1. Decrease the amount of alcohol you are consuming.

Step 2. Try to sip your drink slower, not chug or gulp it down like no other liquid is going to be available to drink ever again.

Step 3. Eat foods with high carbohydrates and fats before drinking, plus adding a little grease to the mix would not hurt either, as these types of food will help reduce your body's absorption of the alcohol.

Step 4. Try taking an over-the-counter anti-inflammatory before drinking if you are prone to headaches.

Step 5. Hydration is critical. Drink plenty of water or a sport drink before drinking. Alternate water or sports drink between every alcoholic drink in order to help you stay hydrated. Also as last resort consume plenty of water or hydrating fluids immediately after drinking alcohol.

Also as a healthy reminder excessive alcohol consumption may cause problems beyond just headaches, so be careful if and when you choose to drink.

Choosing the Best Beer for you

Where can I get good beer?

Depends on what you like, potentially anywhere. Homebrewing, local grocery store, local liquor store, local pub, or straight from the brewery.

Here are a few apps and sites that can help you find your next brew:

Beermapping.com is a project by someone who likes knowing exactly where he is and how far he needs to go for good beer. At this point, there is only one individual working on the code that is making the Beer Mapping Project function. But that one person is supported by many friendly craft beer lovers who offer suggestions for new maps and they help by submitting new locations, adding new reviews, uploading pictures for locations or contributing to the forums.

Untappd is another app devoted to finding beer and rating it after you've found it to help users find the best trending beer near them.

Which beer should I choose in a restaurant?

In this situation, I usually go for a medium bodied ale that is likely to have some fruit-forward notes, will not be as filling or heavy, and has decent alcohol content.

What you don't want to do is blast the bitterness of hops or accidentally pick a sour wheat beer or a sweet lambic. You're probably looking for a decent Blond Ale, Brown Ale, a Bock, Hefeweizen, Red Ale, or Belgian Wit. There are many others that will fit your needs, but if you see any of these on the menu... you're probably going to be A-OKAY. You are also looking at price, because money makes the world go round.

Here are the secrets that only beer industry people know. Most beers by the bottle or even on draft are marked up between 100-400%. The game is to find the best value... the one closest to 100% and furthest from 400%.

You'll have more luck in the middle-high price ranges. The restaurant management has already decided they won't sell a bottle or draft for less than a certain amount, so the lowest priced bottle or draft gets automatically marked up to that amount... even if it costs far less than the next lowest priced bottle or draft. For instance, I've seen cheap bottles marked up more than 800% just to get them up to an acceptable per glass price.

If the restaurant or bar gets a great deal, they are not passing savings along to customers.

So you want to get up past that first tier if you can, where the gains start to get more marginal.

How do I spot a quality beer?

Most people who buy an expensive beer assume they are getting higher quality. There is indubitably some truth to this speculation, once you decide on the amount at which you're investing in a bottle or can, then how do you tell for sure which beers are better than their price peers?

That's where some knowledge of the basic beer regions, styles, laws, and major producers will help you.

On almost every bottle of beer are key identifiers to help you deduce what's inside the glass: Country, Brewery/Brand, ABV%, and it's beer style.

When it comes to beer several signifiers will help you decipher the quality of a particular style, for example with IPAs brewer's use the words "Imperial, Double, or dry hopped" to help describe their brews.

"Imperial" means in beer terms that a beer is higher in alcohol content and bitterness than its traditional version, while "Double" means that it is double the alcohol content and bitterness. "Dry hopping" means that brewers added hops to the brew after fermentation giving the beer a more hop forward taste and aroma.

In your case, you're looking for the beer style, and then the brewery. In general, what I always tell people is you are looking for the beer style that fits your palate, and then if all else is equal, price will begin to actually matter.

Here is a list of the most expensive beers by average price... just in case you want to know:

Samuel Adams' Utopias: $150 per bottle, Most Expensive American Craft Beer

Nail Brewing's Antarctic Nail Ale : $800-1800 per bottle, Most Expensive beer in the World made by animals for animals

Vielle Bon Secours : $1000 per bottle, Most Expensive beer in the World

Brewdog's The End of History: $765 per bottle The Strongest Beer in the World 55% ABV

Which is the best beer brand?

This is a matter of opinion. Basically there are top beer brands growing in each beer style around the world.

There are top brewers in every country. And sometimes the brewers and other people who build up a great brand move to other brands and there is a perceived value that is no longer there.

The list of top beer brands as far as influence starts with Anheuser-Busch/InBev, the producers of Budweiser and Stella Artois, who command a powerful 5% of market share. Snow Beer, a chinese brand of beer, also owns a commanding 5% of market share. Followed by Heineken with about a 2% share, along with Miller and Coors own one percent apiece.[5]

Which country produces the best beer?

Thrillist, an online email newsletter made a list of the best beer by country in March 2015:

1. Belgium
2. USA

---

[5] Bloomberg.com

3. UK
4. Germany
5. Denmark

While the order of the rankings is subject to opinion, it is generally agreed that the following countries produce the best beer: Belgium, Germany, the United Kingdom, the United States, and the Czech Republic are all most commonly found in the Top Five. While the following countries trade spots regularly: Canada, Ireland, Australia, Denmark, and Japan.[6]

What are the most common faults found in beer?

By sheer volume, probably the most common "fault" or "flaw" is skunking and oxidation. Oxidation happens when oxygen reacts to the wort negatively. Which commonly happens when there is too much headspace in the bottle, or before pitching the yeast aeration of the wort. Oxidation causes the beer to taste stale, old, papery, or like cardboard.

---

[6] Thrillist.com, theTopTens.com, BeerAdvocate.com

Often people ask me how long you can keep an open bottle before it goes bad or becomes oxidized. I tell people you have about a couple of hours if left uncovered from the time you pop that tab before it will be boring.

Skunking occurs when the brew comes in contact with too much UV light either during the brewing process or sitting in the bottle on the shelf in direct light. Skunking refers to the aroma that the beer gives off which smells off or like a skunk's spray.

If the brew is extracted from metal brewing equipment that is unprocessed metal then the beer will have a fault of metallic flavoring.

A solvent or plastic-like flavor can occur if faulty plastic equipment is used during brewing as well.

Yeast produces phenols which can give a beer a medicinal taste if they are produced negatively such as; if cleaners/sanitizers are improperly used, incorrect pH levels, incorrect water levels, or incorrect temperature.

A soapy flavor can occur if fermenters and other equipment are improperly cleaned.

A moldy flavor develops if you store beer, wort, or fermenting beer in a damp, dark area, or using moldy grain or malt.

Another flaw is a husky flavor this is also a result of faulty malt.

Cork Taint, sometimes called "TCA" can also develop as a flaw. Basically this is a mold that grows either on the inside of barrels or cork. It creates earthy, musty, moldy flavors and aromas you might find in a dank old cellar or basement wherein a wet dog has been gnawing on wet newspaper. Brewers, of Belgian ales mostly, commonly use corks instead of aluminum bottle caps to close their bomber bottles as well, which can lead to TCA. TCA could possibly happen during barrel aging as well.

Brettanomyces, commonly known as "the Bretts" or "phenolic taint" Brettanomyces is a yeast. It creates some funky smells and tastes like band-aid, horse manure, and rancid cheese or bacon fat. What's weird about this yeast is that brewers of Belgian Style trappist ales or Brett IPAs often include it on purpose. A sour or acidic fault can occur as well due to yeast. A wild or bacterial yeast infection attacks the yeast causing a vinegary, acrid, or sour taste.

If your beer smells or tastes like a struck match, raw sewage, or rotten eggs, you have a sulfur surplus in your brew. This can be naturally produced by yeast during fermentation, Lager yeasts typically create a more overwhelming sulfur-like aroma.

What makes one beer more expensive than another?

Reputation mainly. Usually price increases begin when combining any of the following variables: production costs, smaller batches and limited editions, a respected brewer or brand, consistent quality from year to year, ingredient surplus or scarcity, seasonality, and increasingly the marketing or advertising efforts of new world beers and craft beer.

Keeping and Serving Beer

How to properly pour a beer

Use a clean glass. If you reach for a solo cup, you should probably gift this book to a friend who actually likes beer. But seriously, use a clean one. The oils and other contaminants in a dirty glass will affect the flavor and the aroma of the head, ruining your beer.

Next tip your glass to 45 degrees. Pour directly into the middle of the slope. Once the glass is half full(yes half full, be an optimist, you're drinking beer), bring the glass upright to 90 degrees and pour into the center of the glass. Pour until the head is near 1-1.5" (inches). Some pour longer, purposely spilling over the top while it is tilted, to get more beer in the glass and less head.

How should I store beer?

Shelf-Life

Your average beers have a shelf-life of about 3-6 months before they will begin degrading. However, you can age and keep vintage beers, barleywines, imperial stouts, Belgian strong ales, lambics and old ales. Most decent beers benefit from a year or two of age, while some particular beers can age for as long as 25 or more years.

If you are looking to start your beer cellar, you might want to buy at least two of each beer so you can drink one immediately and then compare it to the one you age.

Upright vs. Laid Down

We polled brewers who pretty much all said to keep your bottles upright as opposed to laid down like wine bottles. In fact, Chimay, one of the top rated brewers in the world, recommends you store their beers upright. Why? Yeast sediment settles at the bottom of your bottle, making the pour much easier.

Temperature

According to Beer Advocate: "Beer benefits from cool constant temperatures; usually around 50-55 degrees F is ideal for most beers, and most beer collectors. Higher temperatures and you'll risk shortening the lifespan of your beer, lower and you'll induce chill haze (cloudy)."

Can I put my beer in the freezer for a few minutes to chill it?

Yes, but be careful not to let it freeze. According to the American Homebrewers Association, freezing beer alters the molecular structure of the proteins in the beverage. It can also reduce the carbonation level and, in the case of bottle-conditioned brew, possibly kill the yeast. And also, beer explodes when frozen. Would you put a grenade in the freezer? No? Then don't let your beer freeze.

How long does beer last?

Google says: 4-6 months, but the truth is that it depends on the storage conditions. It should be kept away from light and between 45-55 degrees F, colder than room temp. You should not keep beer in a pantry for more than 6 months, but in a fridge it could keep up to 2 years. Chances are if you've left a beer in your fridge for that long, you are aging it, or you ain't gonna drink it….

What's the best temperature for serving beer?

Most beers range between 38-50 degrees, so definitely cooler than room temperature. Ales typically can be served between 45-55 degrees, Lagers tend to be served far colder 33-45 degrees, but both tend to be served too cold in general. I suggest keeping your beers in a cool closet out of direct sunlight if not prepared to drink within a couple days.

If you don't have a precise climate control beer fridge, then placing the beer in the fridge for 2 hours before dinner. Imagine you are trying to keep ales in a cellar or cave temperature, and lagers you want to feel like they just came out of a ice cold or snow melt stream near your fancy cave. How many beer snobs would tell you that?

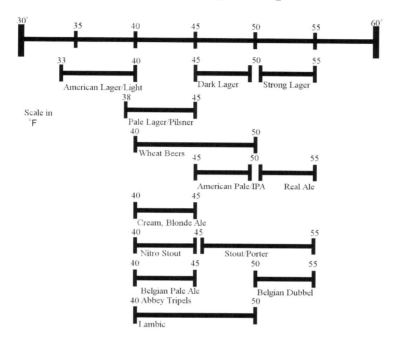

How many bottles of beer are in a case?

It varies based on the brand and distributors ranging from 6 to 30.

What is bock beer?

Bock Beer is a member of the Lager family of German origin from Lower Saxony, though originally an ale is now become almost always a lager.

Einbeck, Southern Germany in Bavaria, claims the origin of Bock beer. Einbeck pronounced Ein- BOCK meaning "Billy Goat", is where the delicious brew derives its name.

Bock means ram or goat in German, which must be where the Spoetzl Brewery in Texas got its mascot for its famous Shiner Bock.

The Bock was originally brewed by Bavarian Monks, during times of fasting such as the Lenten season. The Bock has a higher nutritional content than most beers, giving the monks the extra nutrients needed to make it through their fasting.

Bocks come in a variety of forms such as Dunkel (Dark) Bock, Doppel (Double) Bock, Maibock (Pronounced My-Bock), and Heller Bock.

While Lagers are typically described as thin, clear, subtle, and crisp; the Bock is all of those things, but is darker in color ranging from a light copper to brown, malty and lightly hopped Lager. A Bock should be rich and toasty in both taste and aroma with hints of malt and caramel.

Bocks became popular in the 17th Century due to its extended shelf life therefore allowing it to be shipped to new consumers.

Examples of this style of beer include: *Shiner Bock*: Spoetzl Brewery, *Harpoon Dark*: Harpoon Brewery, and *Bockness Monster*: Ballast Point Brewing Co., *Einbecker Ur-Bock*.

Bocks are also typically associated with the celebrations, holidays such as Christmas, and times of feasting.

Cincinnati, OH is also known to have the largest Bock Beer Festival called Bockfest, celebrating the German-heritage of the city.

What is draught beer?

Draught (or "Draft" if you're in North America) beer is served from a cask or keg instead of in a bottle or can.

The word Draught comes from the Old English word for carrying or pulling beer, "dragan," because before Joseph Bramah's 1797 invention of the first beer pump (which was subsequently used on fire engines to propel water at flames) beer was carried from the barrel to the customer.

You've probably noticed the word "draught" has made it onto some cans and bottles. It turns out Guinness has been making "draught" beer in cans and bottles since the 1960s... which means they include various devices that control the flow of the head of the beer to simulate the draft pull. Some of these devices, called initiators, looked like syringes and required some serious finesse. It wasn't until Guinness unveiled floating widgets in 1997, however, that we started to see plastic widgets inside the cans or bottles.

Can I brew beer at home?

Homebrewing is legal in all fifty states. All of the states have the ability to prohibit the manufacture of beer, mead, hard cider, wine and other fermented alcoholic beverages at home. When prohibition was lifted in 1933, the legislation only lifted the restrictions on homemade wine...beer was still illegal to brew at home. Finally in 1979, homebrewing was made legal by President Jimmy Carter. Most states permit homebrewing of 100 gallons of beer per adult(18yrs and older), per year and up to a maximum of 200 gallons per household annually. In 2013, Alabama and Mississippi were the last to lift the laws prohibiting homebrewing.

How can I make beer at home?

Home brewing kits or a coffee maker. For more on the process, head to chapter 7 for Technical advice, and to Interesting Facts for the full coffee maker brewhack.

Chapter Five - L is for Love

How to Love the Beer in your glass

*"Beer makes you feel the way
you ought to feel without beer"*
- Henry Lawson

The experience of tasting beer begins with picking a brew (or having one picked for you). Because this often gives people the sweats and shame, the sensual experience in beer can start out as a traumatic emotional experience. With your new Palate Identity Profile, you'll easily be able to avoid this by Asking for what you want.

Let's assume you've now got a beer or two in front of you to try... how do you enjoy the experience?

The first step is to clear your pre-judgments. If you can, ignore the beer snob standing behind the bar who is trying to impress you with meaningless words about what you should smell or taste. Let them deal with their own anxiety in whatever way they want, you're here for the fun of an ancient and beautiful alcohol delivery system. Clear your pre-judgments before you pick up the glass and remind yourself that your palate is the only one that matters. You get to have a life where you enjoy every glass of beer that is served to you. I promise, if you do this one step, you will find something to enjoy about almost every glass you encounter. I do, and I've never looked back.

    Now let us discuss HOW to taste a beer. While it can be as easy as taking a sip and deciding to gulp down the contents if deemed worthy or spitting it back out then throwing the glass at the other side of the room in disgust, judges and brewing professionals tend to take a more regimented route that doesn't involve throwing glassware or chugging the contents of the glass.

1. The first step of course is to pour yourself a drink. The pour is as crucial as taking that first sip. When tasting, pour the beer directly into the middle of the glass.

    It is ok if it foams and creates head, it's what you want the beer to do. This releases and unlocks the different aromas of the beverage as well as allows you to judge the foamy head and see the carbonation at work.

When tasting, pour about two to four ounces of beer, this is about quality and tasting not about quantity and getting intoxicated.

2. Second look and admire the color of the beer. check to make sure the carbonation is not sticking to the sides of the glass which is a tell tale sign of a dirty glass. View the head, which is generally agreed-upon as about an inch thick, and look at the forming of the bubbles.

3. Thirdly, smell. Taste with your nose. Stick your nose in the glass and take a huge whiff of that glorious aroma.

   Breathe deeply while you stick your nose deeply into the glass, don't be bashful. Sniff for the smell of the various herbs used, the toastiness of the malt, the bitterness of the hops.

   If it smells skunky or bad, generally that means it was stored incorrectly or UV light damaged the beer. In this hedonistic style of tasting, you are not trying to force the identities of the aromas. You are simply asking yourself, "do I enjoy these aromas?"

4. Finally you may take a sip. Congratulations! You got to the part where you get to consume some delicious alcohol!

Roll that brew all along your tongue so that each taste bud can savor the liquid. Feel how the beverage hits your palate, and decipher the different flavors.

Then if deemed worthy swallow and bask in the finish and aftertaste. Then decide whether or not to have another sip or throw it out. Feel the weight of the ale. Does it feel hot or cool? Does it make your mouth water or your tongue pucker? This is often called the "mouthfeel" and it refers to the weight, viscosity and alcohol content of the beer.

Our tongue is a rather useful tool being able to decipher five distinct qualities; sweetness, bitterness, sourness, saltiness, and umami (savory meatiness).

The action of sipping, you're really not getting much

from the tongue except, "Hmmm, this is good," or "Meh, this is too (sweet, sour, bitter, or meaty) for me." But if you see the action of sipping as also a way of feeling the ale, rather than just sticking your finger in it, you'll get more out of the experience.

After swallowing, breathe in through your nose and out through your mouth, you'll notice that you can taste the brew in the back of your throat. Yes, you have receptors even in your throat that also add to helping distinguish flavor.

5. Lastly, analyze what you have just tried. Take notes on what you recognize and what you've learned from the tasting. Score the beverage using a judging scale or template. Decide what the drinkability of the brew is. Would you drink it again by personal choice or order it again?

    Judging Beer is a little more intense and intricate than just open mouth, pour ale down throat, swallow, and decide if it is good or bad. It is also more than just worshipping the Beer Gods in the hopes they'll show you a sign.

The average person who knows little to nothing about beer will simply taste and decide then and there whether they like it or not. A beer nerd, beer snob, brewer, or beer judge has a set of rules or guidelines they follow when tasting a beer.

- When doing a tasting, you will want to start with your environment. Trying to do a tasting in a noisy club or backyard BBQ is not ideal due to all the opportunities for distractions. In order to do a proper tasting you will want to limit distractions in order to focus all your senses during tasting.

Also try to prevent any unwanted odors from polluting the area, like cleaning supplies, grilled foods, or any other undesirable odors that might affect your senses.

You may also be aware of lighting. Drinking in a dark room does not allow you to see the head of the beer form or enjoy the variety of colors. Also with lighting you want to be aware of the harmful UV light that can cause skunking and ruin the smell and taste of a beer.

- Next consider the glassware you are using for the tasting. Try to be cognitive of the styles of beers you're tasting and what glass best fits the brew. For example a Scottish Ale best fits a nonic pint or snifter glass, where as a Hefeweizen best fits a weizen or flute glass.

- When drinking beer or simply tasting small amounts, have plenty of water available in order to stay hydrated, and food to absorb some of the alcohol.

- As much as I hate to say it, and feel like I am ripping my own heart out, during a tasting or judging event a spit bucket is necessary. It is definitely a party foul to waste beer, but when tasting beers at a competition or even socially, that can become a lot of beer for one person to consume responsibly. Having a spit bucket allows you to pour out the contents of your glass and prepare for the next round, or get rid of a particular bad batch of beer you might not have enjoyed.

- Another task is to keep a tally or score of what you liked and did not like. That way you can keep track of what beers you might want to try again at a later time or one you might want to stay away from in the future.

There are numerous brewing competitions ranging from small setups like Homebrewers to commercial breweries.

The World Beer Cup (WBC) is the largest and most prestigious international brewing competition in the world that happens every two years and was created by the Brewers Association in 1996. This competition acquires two hundred plus highly trained brewing professionals to judge up to ninety different styles of beer. The WBC is known as the "Olympics of Beer Competitions" and is the top of the beer judging world.

The next best competition would be The Great American Beer Festival (GABF) also created by the

Brewers Association. The GABF also provides top notch brewing professionals to judge ninety-two styles of beer. The GABF was established in 1982, and brings together both beer sampling and judging.

Next the American Homebrewers Association (AHA) puts on the National Homebrew Competition which spotlights the ingenuity of the Homebrewer. The National Homebrew Competition functions much like NASCAR in that Homebrewers compete in numerous smaller beer judging events, such as Houston's Dixie Cup, in order to accrue enough points to gain entry to the National Homebrew Competition.

Another notable beer competition is that of the Mondiale de la Biere in Montreal. Also the Beverage Testing Institute (BTI) is an established organization that tastes and scores brews and posts their findings on Tasting.com and in All About Beer Magazine.

How does one become a beer judge you might ask, I mean who doesn't want to be the judge, jury and executioner of a beer tasting?

Well, all you have to do is enroll in the Beer Judge Certification Program or BJCP. The BJCP is the most credible and sanctioned organization for training personnel for homebrewing competitions.

I've included a tasting chart for you to print out and use at your next tasting.

Copyright Owners of *Beer Snobs are Boring*

Beer:			
Brewery:			
Location/Country:			
Glass:			
ABV%:			
IBU:			
Color:			

EYE TEST:

Head:	Not Enough	Perfect	Too Much
Color:	Hazy/Cloudy	Average	Appealing
Carbonation:	Not Enough	Perfect	Too Much

TASTING:

Aroma:	Bad	Neutral	Excellent
Palate:	Bad	Neutral	Excellent
Finish:	Bad	Neutral	Excellent
Aftertaste:	Bad	Neutral	Excellent

Would you drink again?	Yes or No
Would you recommend to a friend/family member?	Yes or No

OVERALL SCORE:

1	2	3	4

NOTES:

The Glassware

Some people will tell you to hold the glass in a specific way. Just remember that your hand is warm, if you want to heat up your beer, hold it by the bowl of the glass. If you want to keep it cold, hold it by the stem or even better yet use a colorful and exciting koozie!

The following is a list of the different beer drinking glasses designed to better enhance the taste of the beer. Some are made to enhance color and the visual aspects of the beer style, others to enhance the aroma, and then some to simply better hold the valuable liquid within. Brewers take their glassware just as seriously as they do when producing the product within.

In fact, Jim Koch, Co-founder and Chairman of Boston Beer Company, had a glass specifically designed for his Samuel Adams Boston Lager.

Flute[7]

The Flute glass much similar to that which you would drink champagne out of is used to enhance and showcase carbonation. The narrowness of the glass allows a quick release of volatiles for a more intense upfront aroma. The long stem of the glass also allows holding the glass without hand warmth affecting the beer.

Styles of Beer used in this glass:

American Wild Ale, Biere de Champagne, Bock, Czech and German Pilsner, Gueuze, Lambic, Vienna Lager, Weizenbock

---

[7] Photo by Flickr/Didriks

Goblet (Chalice)[8]

The Goblet, Chalice, or *Bolleke* is the original classic beer glass. Original made out of horn, then various metals as man progressed industrially, now to glass. The goblet while being smaller in size is great for strong brews. Wide-mouthed for deep sips and designed inward taper concentrates head and aroma, so are designed even to have two centimeters of head. Though mostly goblets are made to be the ornate eye candy of beer glassware.

Styles of Beer used in this glass:

---

[8] Photo by Flickr/Steven Guzzardi

Belgian IPA, Belgian Strong Dark Ale, Berliner Weissbier, Dubbels, Quadrupels, Tripels

Stein[9]

The stein is the classic German glassware, most popularized during Oktoberfest. The Stein is also known as a mug or *Seidel*. This glass is large, heavy, and sturdy. It is

---

[9] Photo by Flickr/a4gpa

also equipped with a handle to prevent hand warmth from harming the delicious brew inside and allowing you to drinking easily from it. This glass is all about holding large volumes of ale and clinking them loudly together with your brethren in celebration of beer. Though ironically it is a big glass for small brews, mainly being used for lagers such as pilsners, helles, and oktoberfest brews.

Styles of Beer used in this glass:

Amber Ales, Red Ales, Blonde Ale, American IPA, American Pale Ale, Bocks, Czech and German Pilsner, Brown Ale, Helles, Marzen (Oktoberfest), Rauchbier, Vienna Lager, English Strong Ale, Doppelbock, and Maibock

Pilsner Glass[10]

The Pilsner glass or Pokal was especially made for the offspring of the Lager, the Pilsner which originates from Plzen, Czech. This glassware is narrow in shape to showcase color, clarity, and carbonation of the beer. The outward-tapered shape of the glass supports and promotes the head of the beer. The Pokal also enhances volatiles. The footed design not only adds stability but elegance to the

---

[10] Photo by Flickr/Steven Depolo

glass, while the stem keeps the hand from warming the liquid. The Pilsner glass is a good general-purpose glass for high-class brews.

Styles of Beer used in this glass:

American Adjunct/Amber/Red/Pale Lagers, American Imperial Pilsner, Bocks. Doppelbocks, Czech and German Pilsner, Happoshu (Japanese Rice Lager), Maibock, Helles Bock/Lager, Vienna Lager, and Witbier

Snifter[11]

The snifter glass largely popularized for brandy and whiskey is also an elegant and classy way to drink a beer. The snifter's wide bulb-like shape yet narrow mouth is used to capture and enhance volatiles and aromas of the beverage. The snifter is ideal for strong ales, barleywines,

---

[11] Photo by Flickr/Steven Depolo

and imperial stouts. The stem also prevents hand warmth and stability of the glass.

Styles of Beer used in this glass:
American and English Barleywines, Double IPAs, IPAs, American and Belgian Strong Ale, Imperial Stouts, Quadrupels, Scottish Ale, Tripels, and Wheat Wine

Stange [12]

A Stange is a traditional German slender cylinder glass. A stange amplifies malt and hop nuances. While being used to serve more delicate beers, it also tightens concentration of volatiles. The glass also forces the user to grip the glass and corrupt the brew with hand warmth.

Styles of Beer used in this glass:

Altbier, Bocks, Czech Pilsners, Gose, Faro, Gueusze, Kolsch, Lambic, Rauchbier, and Rye Beer

---

[12] Photo by Flickr/shankar s.

Tulip[13]

The Tulip glass has become a popular choice for craft beer enthusiasts especially for American IPAs and Double IPAs. The Tulip glass is also known as the *libbey* or *poco grande*. Tulip glasses are a hybrid of a snifter with the mouth or a wine glass. The inward taper of the glass holds

---

[13] Photo by Flickr/Peter Anderson

in the aroma much like a snifter to capture and enhance volatiles and aromas. Yet the outward flare supports large foamy head and fits the lips. While the foot-designed stem prevents hand warmth and adds stability.

Styles of Beer used in this Glass:

American Double IPAs, American and Belgian IPAs, American Wild Ales, Belgian Pale Ales, Belgian Dark Ales, Biere de Garde, Flanders Red Ale, Gueuze, Lambic, Quadrupel, Saison (Farmhouse Ale), Scottish Ale

Weizen Glass[14]

The Weizen glass is the second most popular glassware used in drinking beer outside of the pint glass. Due to the large volume and flute-like shape many bars make the mistake of using the glass simply because it holds a lot of beer and not for tasting purposes.

---

[14] Photo by Flickr/Bernt Rostad

The weizen glass or weissbier vase, has thin walls and is lengthy to show off color and clarity. The glass also allows greater headspace. The large size and inward taper concentrates and holds foam which locks in banana-like and phenol aromas indicative of weizen beer.

Styles of Beer used in this Glass:

American Dark and Pale Wheat Ale, Dunkelweizen, Gose, Hefeweizen, Kristalweizen, Weizenbock

Oversized Wine Glass[15]

Yes, beer even tastes amazing in a wine glass. Unlike wine, beer has a multitude of glassware to enhance the experience you have whilst tasting different brews. I'm sure some fancy wine snob or sommelier upon reading this is having a mental break down at the thought of their

---

[15] Photo by Flickr/Chris Palmer

precious wine glassware being corrupted and used for our beverage of choice.

Though more specifically when tasting beer in a wine glass you should use an oversized one. The use of an oversized wine glass is largely suited for most Belgian Ales. The size allows greater headspace, while the open bowl opens aromas. Plus using one is a great conversational piece, especially when bringing wine drinkers over to the darkside.

Style of Beers used in this Glass:

American Black Ales, American and Belgian IPAs, Double IPAs, Imperial Stouts, American Wild Ales, Belgian Pale Ale, Belgian Strong Dark and Pale Ale, Biere de Garde, Eisbock, English Barleywine, Old Ale, Saison (Farmhouse Ale), Wheat Wine

Pint/Nonic Pint Glass[16]

Last but not least, the Pint Glass. The tumbler, the Becker (German), or quite simply what we would call a normal beer glass. The Pint glass is the most popular glass used by any beverage. It is cheap to make, easy to store and

---
[16] Photo by Flickr/xPrestonx

clean, and even better to drink out of. The pint glass in beer terms has two different fluid ounces depending on which continent you reside in.

In America the pint is 16oz. while the Imperial pint of Europe is 20oz. The pint glass also has an English Brother, the Nonic Pint. The Nonic (Nonick) pint glass resembles any other glass except the small bump just below the lip of the glass. The bump of the Nonic Pint glass protects the glass itself and helps prevent chipping as well as is a grip-of-sorts. Nonic Pints are largely used in England for enhancing the crowning head of English Ales.

Styles of Beer used in this Glass:
ALL

Chapter Six
A is for Adventure

How to plan your Adventure through new styles

"No poem was ever written by a drinker of water."

Homer

Now, it's time to get Adventurous!

First, find yourself some new styles to love. Take the first test of your new tasting skills and find yourself a bar with a bunch of taps near your home. Saddle up to the bar and ask for an adventure. Tell the bartender your palate profile characteristics and ask them to pull you a taste of something new and unique.

This is the easiest way to explore the world because bartenders will honor your palate preference and pour something unique within your styles. Having been this bartender myself many thousand times, I can tell you, this is the best part of the job. You are making someone's day by asking for an adventure.

You may find that Red Ale is actually more your favorite than Brown Ale this way. And then you'll find that a great Extra Strong Bitter actually suits you even more.

Bars/restaurants are better for you in this stage than going to a liquor store and trying to pick your beer off the shelves.

Most of your local grocery/liquor stores have a TERRIBLE-TO-MEDIOCRE selection of beer with only a handful of marginally interesting beers.

Here's why: Your grocery store is part of a huge chain where the sheer amount of product needed to fill shelves would rule out any smaller suppliers or micro-brewers. Given time, this vector produces dressed-up bulk beers that travel and store well - which usually plays against flavor and character (there are obviously outliers, but as a rule the smaller the batch the better).

Your liquor store is tied up with a specific distributor with their specific set of beers they need to sell. They don't take many risks and they do a lot of market research which means they sell to the middle... to the mediocre. So you end up with homogeneous mediocrity. You can find diamonds in the rough... but it'll cost you.

Go to micro breweries and tasting bars and you'll be working with smaller brands and lesser-known styles. Given time, this vector creates beers and experiences that must entice you back with unique quality. Micro breweries and tasting bars also have an on-site curator who is selecting new kegs or beers every week or two. You're almost guaranteed a seasonal ale you've never heard of before. Price also matters a lot less here. You'll be getting solid beer at every price point.

Restaurants can run the gamut... but the bigger the chain, the closer to the grocery store you're going to get.

Next, there is a mid-sized brewery near you... although you may not know it. Find the brewery closest to you and call to ask about their tasting hours and any beer of the month club. They will probably have some great specials, and they may welcome you to a free tasting if you're interested in joining their club.

Another option is to go to the tap room or biergarten near you and just ask questions of the bartenders as much as you can. You will love this experience because it's like finding a secret garden just over your backyard fence. You'll want to take everyone you know to this new and fantastic place you've found. They'll say yes. It'll change your life and the way you look at the area around you.

Next, plan your trip to any of the world's top regions. It wasn't until I'd been to Oktoberfest that I really started to understand the incredible world of high quality beer (and gigantic national song-singing).

1. Oktoberfest – Munich, Germany

Late September to early October (harvest time)

Oktoberfest is a big deal. It's the biggest beer festival in the world, where 6.2 million people drink 6.9 million liters of beer during a 16 day event. It has spawned mini-Oktoberfest celebrations all around the world including in Hong Kong, Vietnam and the largest outside of Germany… in Brazil. If you are in Germany for this festival and you don't get enough, traipse over to Stuttgart for the Constatter Volksfest – which is an autumnal fair that follows a week after Oktoberfest and is the 2nd largest beer gathering in the world.

2. Great British Beer Festival – London, England

Early August

This festival is called the "biggest pub in the world." It is organized by the Campaign for Real Ale (CAMRA) which sets up many other beer festivals in the country. In 2006, CAMRA estimated that one pint is sold every half second at the festival.

3. Great American Beer Festival – Denver, Colorado

Late September to early October

Where Oktoberfest is the biggest… this could be the best beer festival in the world.

Nearly 500 American breweries bring 3000 different beers to the most prestigious judging competition in the USA. According to the Guinness Book of World

Records, the festival is the largest venue for draft beer variety.

4. Great World Beer Festival – New York City, New York

Late October

If you're in New York, find your way into the "United Nations of Beer" where you get unlimited samples from over 100 craft microbreweries.

5. Brussels Beer Weekend – Brussels, Belgium

Early September

This festival honors the "King of Beer" - Duke Jean I, the son of Henri III and Alix of Burgundy, who became a legend in the 1200s as the visionary president of the Brussels Brewers' Guild. Now this festival is organized by the Knighthood of the Brewers' Mash Staff to celebrate the King of Beer and St. Arnold, the patron saint of brewers.

About 200 beers are presented, usually be the brewers themselves - so if you're looking for some pro tips…

What beer festivals have you been to? Or is there one on here that you really want to visit?

Our Additional List of Events Not to Miss

Oktoberfest - Fredericksburg, Texas

Oregon Brewers Festival - Portland, Oregon

Great Australasian Beer SpecTAPular - Various Cities, Australia

Mondial de la Bière - Montreal, Canada

Great Taste of the Midwest - Madison, Wisconsin

Qingdao International Beer Festival - Qingdao, China

Part of the advantage of going on this adventure is you get to see the sources of your beer.

Another big advantage is that you can often meet the brewer or grower (sometimes you may even meet the entire family), and ask questions all day of a person who loves to talk about their beer more than anything else in life... because almost nobody ends up in the beer industry who doesn't LOVE beer.

The more you do this, the more you will learn and love the experience of beer. Again, ask about clubs... you might be able to get into some great arrangements for beer to regularly show up at your front door.

In summary, to plan your adventure you need to know your Palate, Ask questions, and open yourself up to Loving the experience in front of you.

A brief history of beer!

Let me Google that for you: In Mesopotamia (Ancient Iraq), early evidence of beer is a 3900-year-old Sumerian poem honoring Ninkasi, the patron goddess of brewing, which contains the oldest surviving beer recipe, describing the production of beer from barley via bread.

Ancient

Since the history of beer is almost as long as recorded human history, I will only be telling you the highlights.

The earliest known beer was actually an Ale. It was made from a special twice-baked barley bread called *bappir*, which was exclusively used for making beer. It was discovered early on that using the same tub for fermentation yielded more reliable results.

The *Ebla Tablets* discovered in Ebla, Syria show that beer was produced in the city in 2500 BC. There are traces of brewing in Babylonia too. Now for a shocker: Women were commonly the ones brewing the beer, and therefore regarded as priestesses because beer was used regularly in religious practices.

As early as 2100 BC there is evidence that the Babylonian King, Hammurabi, put governing regulations in place for tavern owners. Beer made from barley bread was also part of Egyptian Pharaoh daily diets. The Greeks also made beer, or *Zythos*, and thought it was best in moderation, which of course we practice today so we don't drive our chariots off the road.

Medieval to Early Modern Europe

Hops was written about as early as 736. Flavoring beer with hops was gradually brought into the process, because it was difficult to use the correct proportions. Before hops were used, there was a mix of herbs, called *gruit* (pronounced grew it), but this mix didn't preserve the beer as well.

Gruit was also used as a form of taxation on beer, gruit was monopolized by the priesthood of the catholic church and was sold through the abbeys across Europe.

Beer flavored without gruit spoiled quickly and was not able to be shipped to distant locations. They could have added more alcohol to the beer to preserve it for longer, but that process was too expensive. Hopped beer reached perfection in Bohemia by the 13th century.

Germans pioneered a new level of operation with regulated barrel sizes that made large-scale exportation a reality. This type of production allowed for the start of professional brewhouses, with around ten people involved in production. This type of production made its way into Holland in the 14th century and then into England in the 15th.

Once brewing reached England, the processes of making ale and beer were separated. Ale was made specifically with no hops, herbs or any other similar thing. This is when top-fermenting yeast and bottom fermenting yeast started to take shape.

Asia

While all that was happening in Europe, the Chinese were finding their own early alcoholic beverages, using cooked rice as the grain.

The production of these beverages are still used today, in rice wine and "sake", which is just a general word in Japanese and Chinese languages for alcoholic beverages.

Industrial Revolution

Prior to the Industrial Revolution, all malts were dried over fire fueled by wood, charcoal or straw. This led to all brews having a smokey taste. The hydrometer was invented during this time period.

Before this device was invented, all brewers used the same single malt in their beer. Brown malt for brown beers, amber malt for ambers, pale malt for pale beers. The hydrometer helped to calculate the yield from each malt type.

Pale malt allowed for a higher level of fermentable material, which is why it became the most used malt at the time. In 1817, Daniel Wheeler invented a drum roaster that allowed for creation of dark, roasted malts for porters and stouts. In 1857, yeast's role in fermentation was discovered, which led to improvements to minimize the souring of beer due to microorganisms.

Modern America

The 20th century had a large negative effect on the beer industry as a whole. The consumption of alcohol was continuously seen as unwelcome (bad for the home, prohibition, etc.). The prohibition of alcohol and beer didn't stop it from being consumed, it just forced people to go underground in order to get it.

The number of breweries in the US in 1900 dropped significantly from 1700 or more to less than fifty in 1930 and then jumped back up after prohibition was ended and the world wars took over the world's stage.

After the fighting was over the beer industry stayed steady until the 1980's when the new craft beer culture took effect and brought the number of breweries back up to about 1700 in 2010.

Chapter Seven
T is for Technical

How to Understand the Technical Stuff

"stay with the beer.
beer is continuous blood.
a continuous lover."
- Charles Bukowski

By now, you may have visited a brewery or brewpub and discovered that there's a lot to the process. You might also be enticed to try your hand at homebrewing in your garage. If that's you, and you need to dive in, I understand. I've been there. It's how I decided to get a certification in beer.

This chapter is for you if you're curious about the "How To" of Beers. I'll give you successive levels of the process, but this really is a 101 book, so I'll recommend the next level of reading you should dig into from some venerable authors I respect. This chapter will delve deeper into the intricacies of the brewing process, its ingredients, and answers to more technical questions.

The process in a nutshell:

Barley malt is added to boiling water turning it into wort

Hops are then added to the wort

Yeast is then added to wort turning it into beer

Beer is pasteurized and bottled

Beer is marketed, shipped, and somehow finds its way to your table

Want more detail? Well let us start at the beginning, shall we?

What is Beer?

What is Beer? You mean besides it being a glorious beverage of delicious goodness and the best drink ever? The GREATEST beverage ranging in a variety of colors, flavors, and aromas?

Well since you are reading this book, chances are you've searched the internet for some answers. Google defines beer as "an alcoholic drink made from yeast-fermented malt flavored hops."

If you have read that before or are just now reading this definition you've probably got more questions than answers from that sentence. Let's try again.

Randy Mosher, a leading professional public speaker, teacher, and enthusiast in the beer world, defines beer as "the great family of starch-based alcoholic beverages produced without distillation."

Now we're a little closer but we still need a little bit more information. Beer is made using four major ingredients; barley malt, water, yeast, and hops. Let us add the ingredients to these definitions.

Beer is a starch-based alcoholic beverage produced from using water and yeast-fermented malt flavored with hops without distillation.

Now that we have a definition and know what beer is, do we understand what that actually means? Well let's begin with the brewing process to discover what beer is.

First and foremost, beer is approximately ninety percent water. That's right, good ol' high quality H2O. Water is not zeroed out or purified during the brewing process, the minerals and sediments give the brew flavor and stability. The water is then boiled.

While the water is boiling, crushed malt called *grist* is steeped in the water converting the starches from the malt to sugars. The resulting liquid is called *Wort*.

Now the names of these products were created hundreds if not thousands of years ago, but you'd think our ancestors would've come up with more pleasant and appetizing names than *Wort* or *Grist*.

The wort then goes through *lautering* which is a filtering process to sift out solid grains of malt from the liquid.

The wort, while still at a boil, gets hops added to the mixture. Hops are small, green, pine-cone-looking herbs added for three reasons: flavor, color, and aroma.

The mixture is then sent through a whirlpool to separate the liquid from spent hops, coagulated proteins, and any other solids missed previously. Next the wort is cooled using a heat exchanger before the yeast is added which leads to fermentation.

Fermentation occurs when yeast consumes the sugars in the wort. The by-product of this process is alcohol with a secondary by-product being carbon dioxide causing carbonation.

The wort then becomes our most sacred liquid, BEER! The fermentation process, depending on the style of beer being created, may take anywhere from three days to six months.

The beer may then have carbonation added to it and be pasteurized depending on the beer style, before being bottled or canned.

Then it is shipped out to be consumed.

More About The Ingredients

According to the *Reinheitsgebot* or German Beer Purity Law established in Bavaria 1516, beer consists of four major ingredients that form the brewing recipe; Water, Hops, Yeast, and Malt. The Reinheitsgebot forbids the use of any other ingredients outside of those four previously listed for the sake of purity of the beverage. This law is still in existence today, and forms the basis foundation for the major ingredients in beer.

Water

Not only does it make up a majority of our planet but also in beer. Water in the average beer makes up ninety percent of the liquid composition.

A long, long time ago, in ancient times brewers used their local rivers and waterways to brew. The naturally occurring sediments and minerals that flow through the water helped flavor the beer and distinguish the different brewers apart. Even today brewers pull water from their local water taps for the same purpose.

Water just so happens to be one of the best solvents to dissolve minerals. Now with technological advances brewers can create the ideal water for them by purifying and adding specific mineral mixtures to their water supply for the desired effect. Water used in the brewing process is called, "liquor." The brewing recipe and process starts with water.

Grains

Next grain or malt is added. Water is brought to a boil, and malted barley is then added. Malt Barley contains large amounts of starch which when boiled releases complex carbohydrates and sugars necessary for fermentation. Starch with the help of enzymes, specialized proteins, that convert to sugars. The resulting liquid being wort.

Two types of barley are used most for the brewing process, two-row and six-row barley head. The two-row barley head is commonly used in all malt, ale, and German style beers, they have fatter kernels and grow in colder climates.

The six-row is smaller, but can be grown in warmer climates. The six-row barley is also mostly used in American style beers.

The malt after being picked from the fields and designated for brewing is then either used as a Base malt or toasted, or "kilned." This practice of kilning the malt provides most of the malt flavors, such as kilned malt, Crystal or Caramel Malt, or Roasted Malt. Alas malt barley is not the only grain used in brewing. Adjunct Grains are what these other grains are called.

For large scale commercialized breweries such as Budweiser and Miller who brew large batches at breweries across America, they can not acquire enough barley to brew round the clock day in and day out. So they use adjunct grains, Budweiser mainly using rice and Miller choosing to use corn.

Other adjunct grains such as wheat, rye, oats, and sorghum are also used for specialty brews and craft beer. An example of this would be Oatmeal Stouts, Rye IPAs, witbiers, and Gluten-free sorghum beer.

Hops

After achieving the right wort mixture, Hops are then added during the boiling of the wort to give the brew bitterness and aroma.

Hops are from the *Humulus Lupulus* family of plants. They are a climbing vine similar to that of grape vines but instead of bearing grapes as fruit the vines grow pine cone-like flowers called seed cones or strobiles. The cones are what is known as the hops used in brewing, which contain essential oils and resins.

Hops have been used for over a thousand years, with over one hundred varieties. Germany, England, and America are the top-producers of the plant since hops need moist temperate climates generally between the 35-55 parallels of the north and south hemispheres. Hops are primarily used for adding flavor and aroma due to the alpha and beta acids the cone holds.

Alpha acids are used for antibiotic, bacteriostatic effect, and bitter flavor. While beta acids are used for aroma. These two acids are what is used to distinguish the beer's IBU rating.

Another tactic in using hops is called "dry hopping" which is done after the fermentation process during conditioning to give the brew a more hop forward or front and center bitterness flavor, for you "Hop Heads" who love the bitterness.

Yeast

Found everywhere in the wild and in the lab. A naturally occurring eukaryotic single-celled fungi which reproduce by fission was first discovered by Louis Pasteur in the 1860s is known as Yeast. Yet, Yeast has been realized to cause fermentation since the 1840s.

The adding of the Yeast is the third major step of the brewing process and a major ingredient. Yeast is added to the wort after it is done boiling and after hops are added.

Yeast eats sugars to survive and reproduce, the yeast then converts the sugars into by-products specifically ethanol (Alcohol), CO_2, and small amounts of other flavors and aromas. During the brewing process, Brewers go to great lengths to cultivate their strain of yeast, as well as to protect and grow it.

Yeast is generally used in seven to ten batches before needing to be replaced with a new batch of yeast. There are German breweries that have used the same strain of yeast in their beer for hundreds of years.

Brewers protect their yeast from iron which is toxic to yeast, while adding Zinc to the wort to help promote healthy yeast growth and add nutrients. Also Copper adds nutrients to the yeast so brewers will use either copper piping or add copper during the brewing process.

Most beers are filtered or pasteurized to kill or remove the yeast prior to consumption, but in some beers (like witbiers and wheat beers) yeast remains in the bottle so that the beer can continue to ferment till you pop the top.

Ales typically use yeast deriving from the *Saccharomyces Cerevisiae* strain, and Lagers using the *Saccharomyces Uvarum* and *Saccharomyces Pastorianus* strains.

Carbonation

Carbonation is a by-product of the fermentation process. Carbonation effects mouthfeel, the perception of bitterness, and of course beautiful foamy head. Carbonation is that fizzy taste you feel when drinking a cold brew or drinking a soda.

Carbonation is an unsung ingredient that can also make or break a brew. Too much carbonation and you cannot taste the various flavors, too little and you lose mouthfeel. Another option is to use nitrogen, which gives a foamy head and smaller tighter bubble formation giving it the soft, pillowy look. Also nitrogen is an important substitute for carbonation in draught style beers.

Wild Cards

While Water, Malt, Yeast, and Hops are the four main ingredients used in brewing, brewers use various other ingredients to help customize and make their particular brew unique.

Belgian wits such as Blue Moon use orange peel and coriander. Winter Spices and pumpkin are often used in seasonal Winter and Pumpkin Ales. Fruit is also seen in brewing of Lambics: Framboise uses raspberries, Peche uses peach, Pomme use apples, Krieks use cherries, and Cassis use black currants.

Brewers, like distillers and vitners, use barrels and often trade them between each other. Brewers will use Whiskey barrels to ferment and store their brews creating Bourbon-Barrel aged beers like the Karbach Bourbon Barrel Hellfighter or Harviestoun Ola Dubh whiskey barrel beers.

Once again Brewers stick it to their snobby wine competitors by using their own barrels against them, by using Chardonnay barrels much like using bourbon barrels, Stillwater Brewing makes their Stateside Saison.

Also the Kiuchi Brewery uses Sake Casks to barrel age their Hitachino Nest Extra High beer.

Other various ingredients such as honey, molasses, jalapeno, cumin, star anise, and even sriracha are just a few other examples of the vast variety of ingredients that can be used in brewing to help customize them.

Canned vs. Bottled

While drinking a glass of beer poured from a tap is the best way of consuming the beverage, sometimes a pub or brewery cannot be found. Therefore, leaving the only options left to you being to grab a cold one from the liquor or grocery store where they only sell the delicious beverage in either a can or bottle.

Now while I am sure any enthusiast would love to dive straight into the fermenter and start drinking away or gulp straight out of the tap, consuming this beverage from a can or bottle are great alternatives. But which one is better?

Let's take a look at bottles first. Bottling beer has been around for centuries - long before the can - allowing considerable variation between the two.

Bottled beer comes in four common shapes. Though depending on the brewery and glass blower, brewers have been known to create custom bottles for their brews.

The most common bottle size is the 12 ounce bottle, made to give you one whole beer just for you, because we're adults and we do not have to share.

Next in size are the 22 ounce bottles, also known as a bomber, allowing you to enjoy two full glasses of ale, if your partner in crime wants a taste or your mother tells you that you do in fact have to share.

Following the bombers in size is the 750 milliliter bottle equivalent to that of wine bottles giving you roughly four glasses of the beverage. Another bottle size is the 40 ounce stein bottle, which is known to hold malt beers and is nicknamed a Forty.

Last but certainly not least comes the Growler. The Growler has become a new brew fan favorite allowing a whopping 64 ounces or 1.9 litres of ale. The growler is particularly popular with homebrewers allowing them to bottle their brew in a larger container and store more effectively.

The function of the bottle has three jobs: UV light protection, containment, and portability. UV light and oxidization are the two most harmful things to a beer. Oxidization affects taste, making the beer feel flat and taste like cardboard or stale bread.

UV light causes "skunking." Skunking is the term used to describe the foul stench that is caused by harmful UV light. When selecting from industry standard six pack of beer from either a beer cooler or floor display or shelf select the pack that is in the least amount of direct light. For example selecting from the back of the shelf or cooler. These packs have had the least exposure to light, therefore have the least chance of skunking.

Many beer coolers have fluorescent lights that remain on day and night, therefore the beer at the front of the cooler are most affected by light and often begin to skunk the soonest.

Clear glass bottles, typically used by *Corona*, offer no protection against UV light and simply function as a container and single serving provider. Green glass bottles, such as those used by Dos XX Lager, provide limited protection against UV light being effective about thirty percent.

Brown glass is the most effective of glass bottles being as much as ninety percent effective against harmful UV light. Here is where bottles and cans differ, canned beer is ONE HUNDRED percent effective at preventing UV light.

Due to the aluminum cans design they are more compact therefore allowing more to be packed into a case or cooler.

Two other forms of brew containers include the keg, being the equivalent of a half barrel equaling 15.5 gallons of ale. The other form is a more classic style of brew container called a Cask.

A Cask, barrel, or tun is the original holder of ale. The Barrel holds approximately 160 Liters or 43 US gallons. Production costs and consumer demand has increased so vastly along with the creation and durability of the stainless steel keg has replaced the barrel.

Though purists and enthusiasts alike have found a niche market for what is known as Cask "Real" Ale, meaning that the beer is aged, shipped, and consumed from the barrel, preserving the old ways of consuming ale.

Specific Gravity

No this has nothing to do with the precise measurement of dropping a penny off the Empire State Building as it slams into the concrete creating a miniature crater.

Specific Gravity in brewing refers to the density of the wort or unfermented beer or in other words, how much sugar and other dissolved solids that are contained in the beer.

Measuring Specific Gravity in beer starts with Karl Balling, who although not a brewer, used sucrose solutions and compared percent sucrose by mass to measured specific gravity to the 3rd decimal unit.

Then came Adolf Brix, again not a brewer, who measured the same solutions to the 5th decimal unit. Next came Degrees Plato. By Plato, I mean Fritz Plato, not the greek philosopher. Plato, a German chemist used the Balling and Brix's tables to measure the concentration of sucrose by percentage mass. Degrees Plato shows as a percentage by weight of dissolved solids in the wort by measuring the ratio of water to fermented sugar. So for example 10 degrees Plato equals 10 percent solids. Degrees Plato is typically used by German Brewers as well as Lager Brewers.

Another way specific gravity is measured is Original Gravity. Used by British brewers, Original Gravity measures the ratio of the weight of the wort to the weight of the same amount of pure water. As an example 17 Degrees Plato equals 1070 Original Gravity.

Finding the specific gravity of the wort, or sugar levels in the wort helps brewers establish the levels of alcohol in the brew.

Brewers use two instruments to help them finding these sugar levels: either a refractometer which is a refraction device that measures sugar levels using a spy glass-like device. This device is also used by vintners for measuring the sugar levels in grapes.

The other instrument used is a Hydrometer. A hydrometer looks much like a thermometer, it is a glass tube that floats in the wort and is used to measure the density of the wort giving a specific gravity.

Standard Reference Method

I am sure if you have ever picked up a beer menu at your local pub and perused the synopses of the brews available or even happened to notice on the side of a bottle or two the SRM rating and wondered, "What the hell is SRM?"

SRM stands for Standard Reference Method, which is a system that Beer Judges and Brewers use to scale and compare beer and malt color. SRM varies between a red and yellow color scale, the lowest score being a 2 which is a SRM color of Pale Straw and the highest score being a 40 or higher with the SRM color of Black.

The American Society of Brewing Chemists, or ASBC, oversees analytical standards for brewing in the USA and sets the standards for SRM. While their European counterparts, The European Brewing Convention or EBC does the same abroad.

Though both organizations are separate entities and therefore do not have a generally agreed-upon verbal description of color scale, the EBC is about twice as high as the ASBC scale.

Beer color scaling was created by a British Brewer Joseph Lovibond, who lived during the late 19th century, and after failing at gold mining went to work in his family's brewery.

When you invent something revolutionizing you get to name it after yourself, Degrees Lovibond was the first way in which brewers compared beer color. Using a colored glass stereoscope-like device called the Lovibond Comparator, brewers and judges would flip through various colored glass slides until the glass matched the color of beer.

Another way brewers compare beer color is using a Tristimulus colorimeter which measures in the same red, green, and blue wavelengths as our eyes.

EBC = (SRM x 1.97) ASBC

ASBC SRM Scale
0- 2 - Pale Straw
3 - Straw
4 - Pale Gold

6 - Pale Amber

9 - Medium Amber

12 - Deep Amber

15 - Amber Brown

20 - Brown

24 - Ruby Brown

30 - Deep Brown

40+ - Black

IBUs

IBU stands for International Bittering (or Bitterness) Unit and it is used to gauge the bitterness of beers.

In more precise terms, it describes the quantity of alpha acids from hop resins that have been isomerised by boiling wort. The unit of measure is parts per million, or milligrams per litre.

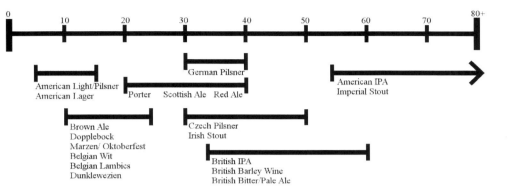

Chapter Eight
E is for Education

How to get more Education if you want it

"They who drink beer will think beer" - *Washington Irving*

Education methods:

1. Books, Magazines and Online Learning

2. Travel, Tasting, and Events

3. Certificate and Degree Programs

4. Homebrewing

Method 1: Books, Magazines and Online Learning

There is a lot that can be learned about beer. You are currently reading just one of the many books on beer and brewing. While ours is more of an introduction about finding your palate and giving a foundation of learning, some books will go much deeper into details on more specific subjects.

Reading about beer is fun anytime, but the best part about these methods is you can read anywhere. Planes, trains and automobiles (you should probably not operate heavy machinery while reading though). Or you can read from the comfort of your own home, because who wants to wear pants anyway?

A good book to start with is "The Complete Beer Course." A personal favorite and Editors choice - "Tasting beer," by Randy Mosher. For those who just have to have a device in their hands all the time there are also blogs and vlogs you may like. The Beer magazine covers a plethora of topics you may want to read further on, as well as All About Beer Magazine.

5 Books to Read

(in order of recommended progression)

1. Tasting Beer - Randy Mosher
2. The Complete Beer Course -Joshua M. Bernstein
3. The Oxford Companion to Beer - Garrett Oliver
4. The Brewmaster's Table - Garrett Oliver
5. How to Brew- John Palmer

Top 5 Magazines

(in order of recommended progression)

1. DRAFT Magazine
2. BeerAdvocate
3. All About Beer
4. Ale Street News
5. Taps: The Beer Magazine

Top 3 Blogs

If you are a blogophile, there are probably some great ones that focus specifically on your beer and brewing interest. You can learn some great things from these sources from experts and average joes alike, and they're often good resources to connect with via social media.

1. Beer Street Journal
2. The Full Pint
3. Beer Month Club

Method 2: Travel, Tasting, and Events

The fastest way to learn is definitely the most interesting: beer tastings.

Participating in a beer festival can give you a taste of the wide variety of beers out there. You can learn what you like and what you don't without wasting money on a whole beer or a whole 6 pack. Also you have a chance to mingle with fellow brewing enthusiasts, brewers, and learn about various breweries. Chances are that the people handing you those delicious beers in your tasting glass will know a lot about what they are serving. The craft beer community is also a helpful one. If their beer is not what you are into, they will help you find one. Make sure you have a ride home, the Greeks have been preaching moderation since they discovered this magical medicine in ancient times.

Traveling is definitely more expensive, but can give much more depth. Other countries have a much longer and richer heritage than America and have been brewing just as long.

They have had time to perfect and adjust their recipes as they see fit. It will be far easier to get beer specifically from that country, within that country.

Anywhere you go, there will be imports, but visiting that country and/or region will give you a better understanding of that style of beer.

Method 3: Certificate and Degree Programs

Any of this information will be for those interested in the next steps of beer and brewing. The first certificate program that comes to most beer drinkers mind is the Cicerone certification program.

They have 3 levels: Certified Beer Server, Certified Cicerone, and Master Cicerone. These certifications are specifically written for the server to educate the drinker, or at least give enough information to make an educated decision.

Next we have the Beer Judge Certification Program. The BJCP is a non-profit organization that strives to educate judges for homebrewing competitions. This program is for the people who are geeks and interested in going the extra mile for the community. This program will include how to taste off-flavors (things that shouldn't be there), techniques in brewing, as well as the final product.

There are an unlistable amount of brewing and beer tasting classes offered by a wide range of community colleges to brewing schools such as the Siebel Institute of

Technology in Chicago, IL or the Technical University of Munich in Munich, Germany.

Check your local colleges for where you might attend some of these classes and go from there.

Professional Brewing Schools & Courses

1. American Brewers Guild - Salisbury, VT
2. American Society of Brewing Chemists - St. Paul, MN
3. Master Brewer's Association of the Americas - St. Paul, MN
4. Siebel Institute of Technology & World Brewing Academy - Chicago, IL

Universities and Degree Programs

1. Appalachian State University - Boone, NC
2. Auburn University Graduate Certificate - Auburn, AL
3. Central Washington University - Ellensburg, WA
4. Cal Poly Pomona - Pomona, CA
5. Metropolitan State University of Denver - CO
6. Olds College Brewery - Alberta, Canada
7. Oregon State University - Corvallis, OR

8. Regis University - Denver, CO
9. UC Davis - Davis, CA
10. UC San Diego Extension - La Jolla, CA
11. University of the Sciences - Philadelphia, PA
12. University of Wisconsin Stevens Point
13. Western Kentucky University - Bowling Green, KY
14. University of Sunderland - Sunderland, UK
15. Campden BRI - Surrey, UK
16. Doemens Academy - Munich, Germany
17. Heriot-Watt University - Scotland, UK
18. Institute of Brewing & Distilling - London, UK
19. Niagara College - Ontario, Canada
20. The Scandinavian School of Brewing - Copenhagen, Denmark
21. VLB Berlin - Berlin, Germany
22. Weihenstephan - Freising, Germany

Method 4: Homebrewing

A more expensive way to taste test is homebrewing. There are a few main types of brewing kits, malt extracts and full mash are 2 of the most common. Malt extract kits usually come with 1 or 2 cans of liquid and a large container. You basically just combine the cans into the container and add some hops and seal.

The full mash method is for serious homebrewers only. There are so many variables to consider when trying to brew the beer your tastebuds are longing for, but will be extremely rewarding when you do get it. I recommend starting with easy kits and moving up. You will certainly learn a lot in this process and can be a very fun experience. Be sure to know and follow your state or counties homebrewing regulations.

Guilds and Societies

There are groups or guilds in your area that will be meeting in a weekly or monthly rotation. Reach out and ask them whatever questions you have. Again the beer community is usually helpful and WANT to share their information with you.

Also try out the following organizations and social groups; Brewer's Association (BA), American Homebrewing Association (AHA), BeerAdvocate, The Brewing Network, Home Brew Talk, Untappd, and Craftbeer.com.

Summary

You should have learned some things whether you skimmed this book and looked at the pictures, or if you were a good student and read every word (wow, you're a better person than I am).

We hope you'll leave us a nice review on Amazon, and that you'll share this with friends so we can continue to brace ourselves against the beer snobs.

Interesting Facts To Stump the Snobs

Take these bad boys out at a party and watch everyone fall in love with you.

- Water destined for brewing is called "liquor", and English apprentices were fined tuppences for calling it water.
- The Pilsner was born in 1842 in Plzen, Czech Republic.
- George Washington owned his own Brewhouse that was located on Mount Vernon.
- Cenosillicaphobia; the fear of an empty beer glass.
- Oenophobia; the fear of wine.
- Zythology; the study of beer and beer-making (brewing)
- Hops and Marijuana are in the same plant family.
- Weihenstephan is the oldest functioning brewery having been established in 1040.

- Women were the first professional brewers, these women were known as Brewsters and were considered the most noble and beautiful women.
- In the middle ages, beer was consumed more than water. The beer that was brewed was safer due to most microorganisms being killed during the brewing process and by the alcohol.
- The average American consumes about 23 gallons of beer a year per capita, while the average Czech consumes about 40 gallons a year, we got some catching up to do.
- North Dakota consumes the most beer per capita about 44 gallons out of all the 50 states, doubling that of Utah the next closest state at almost 20 gallons.
- Brewmeister's Snake Venom is the strongest beer in the world coming in at 67.5% ABV.
- More Guinness beer is consumed in Nigeria than actually drank in Ireland.
- It's a US law that people cannot be shown consuming an alcoholic beverage on TV. Therefore in Beer commercials brands aren't allowed to show people actually drinking the beer.

- In 1922, when the Nobel Prize was won by the scientist Neils Bohr, the Carlsberg brewery gave him a perpetual supply of beer piped into his house.
- In 1814 London, a huge vat ruptured in the parish of St. Giles causing almost 400,000 gallons of beer to flood several streets and killing eight people.
- The First documented use of hops was in the 11th century by Germans, and first being cultivated in 736. Pepin III (Charlemagne's Father) grew hops in his private garden. In 1629 hops were first grown in the US by English and Dutch Settlers.
- Keg Theft: $50+ million lost each year, with some 350,000 stainless steel kegs in circulation averaging to be $150 and rising due to steel prices. Criminals steal the kegs to trade in for the steel, while on the less criminal side homebrewers and college kids simply think that by paying a deposit fee and then just keeping the used kegs shells is the same as the purchase price (it is not).[17]
- Some archeologists suggest that civilization may have been founded specifically for the production of beer

---

[17] http://www.beerinstitute.org/policy-issues/keg-theft

- The porter is named after the day-laborers of the time, which were called "porters."
- Ice Beers: a type of strong lager brewed at subzero temperatures so that ice crystals form. The beer typically has low-moderate body with a trace amount of residual sweetness because it is more condensed. Eisbocks are the older brother to German Doppelbocks. These beers are generally dark in color, almost black, ranging from 9-14% ABV. Unfortunately, these beers are extremely hard to come by in the U.S.
- Can I get beer in the mail? Short answer: yes. It is technically illegal, but there are ways to get around it. Companies who know they are shipping beer to you will require you to be present for delivery. The regular parcel shipping companies will ship your beer if they don't know it is beer. Basically, if you package it so it won't break and spill, they won't bother to open it. If it does happen to leak, they will open it, and they will toss the entire box with no refund.
- What are dry beers? Dry is an adjective that can be used to describe any beer (or any fermented beverage low in residual sweetness). However, in modern usage, Dry Beer usually refers to a specific style of extremely

highly attenuated pale lager popular in Japan and briefly popular in the United States as well.
- "Pale ales" of old were not actually pale, they were just lighter in color than the usual stout or porter that was most commonly drank. The Pale Ales were actually more amber or darker in color.

BONUS: How to brew beer in a coffee maker

1. Gently break the shell of the malt
2. Place the grains into the coffee pot. Now pour filtered water into the coffee maker and turn it on. Let it do its business. The coffee maker will keep the liquid at a nice constant temp.
3. Strain the grains out of the liquid, then pour it into the machine. Leave the grains in the filter. Add one cup of water into the chamber with the liquid. Flip the machine on. Let it run through. Turn the machine off and repeat the process of adding one cup of water. Repeat five times.
4. The liquid you have just created is your wort. Place the wort in a saucepan, bring the wort to a rolling boil. After 20 minutes, add 5 to 7 hop pellets to the

wort and boil for another 30 minutes. Stir the pot, bringing the extra sediments off the sides of the pot back into the wort.

5. Next pour the liquid carefully into your canning jar. DO NOT SPLASH. It's hot and could burn you, but worst of all it will mess with the flavor of the beer. Adding contaminants from the air can and will affect the taste.

6. Now that you have carefully poured your sweet sweet beer into the jar, place it in a sink full of cold water. Let it cool until the temperature of the liquid is between 60-70 degrees.

7. Screw the top on and shake vigorously. This will aerate the wort.

8. Now add your yeast. This jar is your fermentation tank. After you add your yeast, screw the top on and place in a cool dark place for a week. This sweet liquor will become beer in that time.

References

- Cicerone.org
- Craftbeer.com
- Beer Advocate (beeradvocate.com)
- HomeBrewTalk.com
- BeerGuru.com
- All About Beer Magazine (AllAboutBeer.com)
- RateBeer (RateBeer.com)
- Tasting Beer - by Randy Mosher
- The Complete Beer Course - by Joshua Bernstein
- The Brewer's Apprentice - by Greg Koch and Matt Allyn
- How to Brew: Everything you need to know to brew beer right the first time - by John J Palmer
- The Brewmaster's Table - by Garrett Oliver
- The Ultimate Book of Beers - by Mark Kelly & Stuart Derrick
- Brewer's Association
- Beer Institute
- American Homebrewing Association

Also by Dale Thomas Vaughn

FICTION
Fatal Breach

Action/adventure novel about purpose, fate, romance, brotherhood, and holding on to the seat of your pants.

Dr. Mann's Kind Folly
AMAZON BEST-SELLER

A sci-fi novella about Dr. Mann, a time-traveling, jetpacking, mad scientist in an intense moral dilemma.

NON-FICTION
Wine Snobs Are Boring
AMAZON BEST-SELLER

Identify your unique wine palate so you are never lost in the wine aisle or stressed by the wine menu ever again.

The 10-Minute Memoir
AMAZON BEST-SELLER

This book came from a deep heartfelt desire to know the stories of my family. Write Your Memoir In Just 10 Minutes A Day With This Easy Q&A Journal

Connect with Us

Dale:

www.Facebook.com/DaleThomasVaughn

or

www.Twitter.com/NextGent

Shae:

Twitter.com/VaughnS13

Daniel:

Twitter.com/SouthernYankee9